A Histor

A History of
Ilsington

Bill Ransom

Phillimore

2005

Published by
PHILLIMORE & CO. LTD
Shopwyke Manor Barn, Chichester, West Sussex, England

ISBN 1 86077 351 6

Printed and bound in Great Britain by
MPG BOOKS LTD
Bodmin, Cornwall

CONTENTS

ACKNOWLEDGEMENTS

I wish to thank primarily the late Dick Wills of Narracombe Farm for encouraging me to write this history, for giving freely of his detailed knowledge of the parish and for bequeathing to me much of his extensive library of books and manuscripts collected over a lifetime. My thanks also to my daughter, Valerie, for her encouragement, for the photos accompanying the text and for the translations from the Latin.

Others who have contributed data or assisted in a more general way are Dr Burt of Exeter University, Mr Cullen of Leighon House, Malcolm Ford of the Rora Christian Fellowship Trust, Mr E. Fursdon of Fursdon Lacey, Geoffrey Hill of Ilsington, John Hobbs of Tavistock, Mrs McIlroy of Rora Farm, Lord Munro of Langholm, Mr and Mrs Perrin of Ashburton, Peter Thomas of Exeter Cathedral Library, Yvonne Ware-Owen of Ilsington, Michael Wills of Lymington and Mrs and Mrs Sawrey-Cookson of Bagtor House.

Last, but by no means least, I wish to thank the staff of the Devon Record Office and of the Westcountry Studies Library for their courtesy, patience and help over many years.

LIST OF ILLUSTRATIONS

Plates

Figures

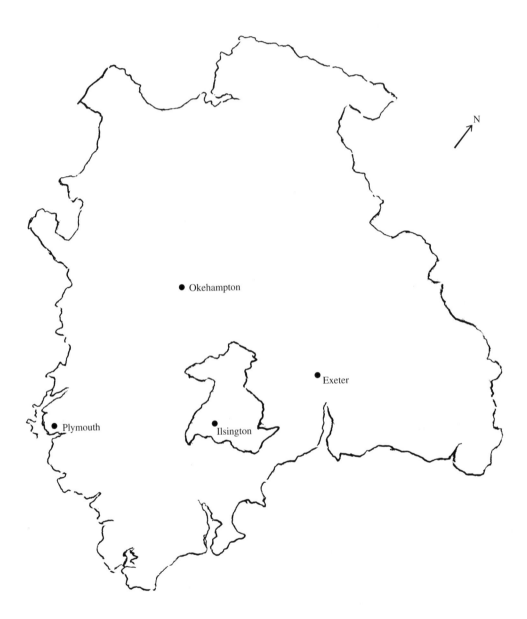

N

● Okehampton

● Exeter

● Plymouth

● Ilsington

Fig. 1 *Position of Ilsington parish within Devon and the Hundred of Teignbridge.*

INTRODUCTION

Ilsington parish lies in the county of Devon some fourteen miles south-west of Exeter and six miles west of Newton Abbot. Bovey Tracey is three miles to the north-east. The parish boundaries adjoin those of Manaton, Widecombe, Ashburton, Bickington, Ogwell and Newton Abbot. It is in the hundred of Teignbridge, the county district of Newton Abbot, the rural deanery of Moreton and the diocese of Exeter.

With the extinction of the mining, quarrying and pottery activities of the 19th and early 20th centuries, it has become again a primarily agricultural parish, although few of the inhabitants are now directly employed on the land. Many work in neighbouring areas, particularly Bovey Tracey, Newton Abbot, Exeter and Torbay, and many are retired. The latter have often come from the counties bordering London in search of a more peaceful and spacious environment (within the parish there are some three acres per person). The influx of such retired people has often led to the expansion and refurbishment of the homes bought, and this in turn has helped support and often create small local firms undertaking building, decorating, plumbing, heating, electrical services, gardening, hedge and tree-cutting and such like.

The northern end is a gateway to Dartmoor. Haytor Rocks, Rippon Tor, Saddle Tor and Holwell Tor are all within the parish and the Dartmoor National Park and attract many visitors every fine weekend and throughout the summer. The highest point is the summit of Rippon Tor at 1,564 feet and the lowest Drum Bridges at 65 feet. The climate reflects these changes in altitude with lower temperatures and greater rainfall the higher one goes. (Temperature falls by around 1.6 degrees centigrade with every 1,000 feet. My house at some 860 feet above sea level has an annual average rainfall of some 1,450mm.) Two small rivers, the Sig and the Lemon, flow from the vicinity of Haytor Rocks to join near Sigford, where they are also joined by the Langworthy Brook. The parish has not been the site of nationally significant events; there have been no bloody battles fought here. Its history has been relatively tranquil with a typically rural reaction to national changes: a little slow and generally conservative but never radical. It has, however, a history underwritten by documentary evidence of nearly 1,000 years and through archaeology of well over 3,000 years which is worthy of being recorded and the following is an attempt to do so.

I

PREHISTORY

Palaeolithic man, if he ever trod the area later to become the parish of Ilsington, left no traces of his passage as he did in Kent's Cavern in Torbay. Tool finds in that limestone cave provide firm evidence of his presence there at least 100,000 years ago during the Ice Age of the Quaternary period. Probably caves such as Kent's Cavern and at Brixham, in which evidence of palaeolithic man was also found, provided shelter from the climate which at times included very cold phases (although Devon was never engulfed by an ice sheet).

Some 10,000 years ago the climate became much milder and about 8,000 years ago a big rise in sea level drowned the land bridge to the continent. During this period the evidence for the presence of mesolithic man in Devon and the south west, through the tools left behind, becomes substantial. In Ilsington we seem to have the first signs of his passage here. Pettit in 1974 wrote of the discovery of a flint some three inches long of mesolithic age, presumably a microlith, found near Holwell Tor and later housed in the Exeter Museum. While this can no longer be located, there is no reason to doubt the authenticity of the statement. The hunter-gatherers in the early mesolithic period probably numbered no more than ten to twenty thousand throughout the whole of the country and their presence, even fleetingly, in the Ilsington area would have been a rare event. The forests in which they hunted were largely of oak and hazel with some pine and birch.

The life style in mesolithic times gradually gave way to the acquisition of farming and related skills which offered a better potential for steady development and are the hallmark of neolithic peoples. Near the source of the river Sig, below Saddle Tor and the road to Widecombe, at SX 7576 7640, are the remains of a tomb believed to be late neolithic or early Bronze-Age and belonging to a class known as 'entry graves'. (These are among the oldest remains on the moor, the best known examples being at Corringdon Ball, Cuckoo Ball and the Spinster's Rock, Drewsteignton and dating from 3000 to 2000 B.C.) The Sig remains have not been dated but an origin around 2000 to 1500 B.C. would not seem to be greatly adrift. The remains comprise a circular mound about four metres in diameter surrounding a rectangular chamber about three metres by 1.4 metres. There is no capstone but the side slabs remain. The entrance is oriented south by east. It was only in 1982

1 *Tomb at Sig Head.*

that the remains were recognised as being of this class of tomb. It must have been rather more distinct then for now it is well covered with gorse and other vegetation and quite difficult to find and, once found, to interpret its type. Another artefact of this period may be the adze found in the bed of the river Sig in 1978. This was 280 mm in length with a maximum blade width of 55 mm and composed of an altered metamorphic dolerite, almost certainly a hornfels. There is no knowledge now of its whereabouts.

The parish, while not rich in prehistoric remains which make immediate impact, contains within two parallel reaves a large area of huts and Celtic fields. Reaves are boundary walls and may demarcate individual fields and farms, entire settlements and even major territorial divisions. Many reaves are medieval but Dartmoor is rich in those built around 1500 B.C. In later years the lines of reaves were often followed by superimposed hedges and walls. The settlement is part of what is known as the Rippon Tor system and brackets the tor, running over the commons of Horridge, Mountsland and Halshanger. Horridge and part of Mountsland lie within Ilsington parish and Halshanger and the other part of Mountsland in Ashburton parish. Within Ilsington parish there are the remains of at least 18 circular huts with diameters ranging from 4 to 8.1 metres. Wall heights range from 0.5 to 1.3 metres but are generally about 1 metre; some of the huts have double walls. They lie mostly to the south-east of Rippon Tor and in an area from SX 7566 to 7586 and SX 7418 to 7488, that is an area about 700 by 200 metres. The whole system including that part in Ashburton parish may have been the largest in Britain, its boundary to the south being lost now in modern farmland. In 1964 a rough track was made through the site to facilitate the removal of timber from Bagtor Woods. A Mr Hopkins of Risca, Monmouthshire found a bronze palstave by the track at about SX 7576 7436. The palstave has a blade length of 130mm and a width of 28mm with a constriction at the base of the blade giving a butt width of 22mm. It does not belong to the British series of Bronze-Age palstaves but is believed to be an import from the continent and to date to between the 14th and 12th centuries B.C. It is now in Exeter Museum.

A further settlement lies just to the east of Smallacombe Rocks, SX 7563 7824. Four huts can be seen and are of particular interest in that they are the only huts within the parish to have been excavated. This was done in 1894 by the Dartmoor Exploration Committee. The largest of the four huts had a diameter of about nine metres, with double walls one metre thick packed between with earth and small stones.

Finds included a flint knife, a dense slaty stone used for rubbing down seams on skins, charcoal and some sherds from clay pots, the sherds being found in three of the four huts. The best pieces, from the largest hut and highly ornamented with a twisted cord pattern, came, it is believed, from two cooking pots, one of which would have been of some 300 mm in diameter. The pots were made from a reddish-brown paste which was permeated by some black carbonaceous matter. The remains of perhaps two fireplaces were also found. Further settlements lie a little to the west of the Sig chambered cairn and consist of four hut circles, the largest pair of diameter seven to eight metres, in an area between the Becka Brook, Holwell Tor

2 *A Smallacombe hut circle (Haytor Rocks can be seen in the background).*

and Emsworthy Rocks and to the west of Pinchaford, in Bagtor Woods and on Bagtor Down. Much of this last area was extensively worked for tin and the prehistoric field banks were damaged, the remains consequently being difficult now to identify. Agricultural settlements on Dartmoor, although started in the Bronze Age, continued into the first phase of the Iron Age and one such can be seen below Rippon Tor at SX 7517 7571 consisting of three fields in some 1.06 acres. All the circular huts are likely to have had a central post or a ring of posts supporting a thatched conical roof.

Cairns are mounds mostly of stone and mark graves of people presumably of importance in their day. The term 'barrow' is sometimes used synonymously, though more correctly when the mound is formed predominantly with soil. Cairns and barrows were built over a long period spanning both the neolithic and Bronze Ages and were of ritual significance. Just within the parish boundary on Rippon Tor is one of the largest cairns on Dartmoor, some 28 metres in diameter and four metres high. Two smaller cairns lie a little to the south east and two others each about 20 metres in diameter a further 100 metres away. Seven Lords Lands cairn is just north of Hemsworthy Gate

3 *Bronze-Age cairn on Rippon Tor.*

4 *Owlacombe barrow.*

on the boundary line of the parish. This is about 10 metres in diameter with a kerb of surrounding stones which has kept the cairn in a good state of preservation. Further cairns lie on Horridge and Mountsland commons and south-east of Haytor Rock below the road to Widecombe, the last being much damaged. Indeed, following plundering through the ages, often for building stone, the present appearance and size of cairns may be only representative of the original. Ring cairns are near-circular banks of small stones surrounding an interior often only slightly raised. There are examples at SX 7673 7810 and in that vicinity, the largest being about 21 metres diameter with a bank 0.4 metres high and 1.5 metres wide. Owlacombe Barrow (marked 'burrow' on the standing stone there) may well have been the 'ruwan beorgh' on 'Peadingtun' landscaro (see Chapter II). There is no sign now of a barrow ever having been here but an outcrop of rock standing well above the surrounding ground may have been mistaken for one. None of the cairns or barrows within Ilsington parish have been formally excavated but the majority of cairns and barrows elsewhere on Dartmoor have revealed an empty pit, although a few have shown the presence of a cist, a little charcoal and occasionally a flint chip.

There are other hut circles, cairns and barrows too numerous to mention in this book but they are entered in the Devon County Sites and Monuments Register and Pearce lists a 'celt' (a sharp edged tool) and an axe found in the parish, both of the Bronze Age. The fact that the open moor has not been cultivated would have allowed these remains of early man still to be seen today. At lower levels there may well have been more which has been ploughed or cultivated so leaving no physical signs. Place-names can often suggest the likelihood of their earlier existence. In the parish near Lounston and Lenda are fields called Stone Barrow and Higher and Lower Borough, which may be examples.

II

THE SAXON AGE

There are no known Roman or Saxon remains in the parish but the fact that the Saxon tribes did leave their mark is shown by the place-names from which many of the current names derive. Thus Ilsington itself has its derivation in the personal Saxon name Aelfstan. Other probable examples are Bacga's torr (Bagtor), Aegenoc (Ingsdon), Sicga's ford (Sigford) and Puneca's ford (Pinchaford).

The function of reaves in demarcating boundaries has already been referred to and they are important in helping to suggest the possible line of a Saxon boundary known as the landscaro of Peadington. The strip of parchment defining this boundary is written in Anglo-Saxon and is believed to be part of an episcopal charter dating to A.D.1050 at the latest. It may have helped establish later the boundaries of the parishes of Ilsington, Ashburton, Bickington, Widecombe and Woodland. The parchment shows the boundary as starting and finishing at the place where the river Ashburn falls into the river Dart. This is one of the few places quite clearly identifiable but, unfortunately, most of the rest are places no doubt well known in their time but described in terms too general to help the reader today, such

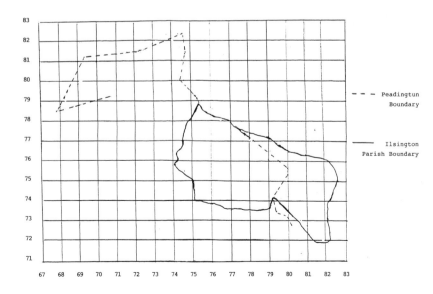

– – – Peadingtun Boundary

——— Ilsington Parish Boundary

Fig. 2 *Map of the Peadington boundary and the Ilsington parish boundary.*

5 *Bickington/ Ilsington boundary stone.*

as, 'the hive tree', 'the spring' and so on. Nevertheless, many attempts have been made to relate these to places known today based on local knowledge of the topography. The following is one more suggestion, but relates only to where the line of the landscaro may enter, pass through and leave the parish of Ilsington. Davidson's transcription of the Anglo-Saxon wording has been adopted.*

Of cealffa dune on sufonstanas (from calves down to the seven stones). From Two Barrows on Hameldon, SX 707792, down to Soussons, SX 678786, where there is still a stone circle.

Of sufonstanum on hyfan treow (from the seven stones to the hive tree). Probably close to Headland Warren, SX 693812.

On hyfan treow on hord burh (from the hive tree to the treasure fort or fortified place). To King's Barrow, SX 709814.

Of hordbyrg on deoford (from the treasure fort to the deer ford). Perhaps to near Vogwell, SX 723816.

Of deoforda on langestan (from the deer ford to the longstone). Either to Langstone Cross or Langstone in Manaton parish SX 746824.

Of langa stane on eofede tor (from the longstone to the ivied, or ivy tor). To Manaton Rocks, SX 747815.

Of eofede tor on hean dune forewearde (from the ivied tor to the forepart of High Down). To Hayne Down.

Of hean dune on thone blindan wille (from the high down to the blind well). To a well in the vicinity of SX 752792.

Of tham wille on writelanstan (from the blind well to the inscribed stone). To near Hole Rock, SX 756785.

Of tham stane on ruwa beorh (from the inscribed stone to the rough mound). To Owlacombe Barrow, SX 776776.

Of ruwan beorgh on fyrspenn (from the rough mound to the furze hill). To the vicinity of Penn Wood.

Of fyrspenn on wyrt cumes heafod (from furze hill to the head of the herb valley). To near a Bickington/Ilsington boundary stone at SX 792741.

Of wyrtcumes heafde on rammeshorn (from the head of the herb valley to Ramshorn). Here at last is another certain position, Ramshorn lying at SX 793734.

Of rammeshorne on lulca stile (from Ramshorn to Lurcombe).

The Saxon boundary now passes away from Ilsington parish and is not considered further here.

* The reasons for this interpretation are given by the author in an article in the *Devon Historian*, no. 65 (2002).

III

ORIGIN AND GROWTH

A parish in early times was an area served by a church with a resident priest. Ilsington originated as a typical ecclesiastical parish certainly as early as the 12th century but its boundary was largely determined before that. Civil parishes originated in Tudor times when Poor Law and highway legislation made them units of local government, the civil and ecclesiastical boundaries have not always been coincident. From time to time the boundary of Ilsington parish was 'beaten' by local residents to establish its validity. The first known beating of the bounds is recorded in the churchwardens' accounts for 1785 when a payment of £5 7s. 2d. was made for 'Twise vuing the bounds of ye parish'. There may well have been earlier viewings. Of course, the boundary was often disputed here and there by neighbouring parishes. The present civil boundary of Ilsington parish, now generally accepted, was adopted after the Ordnance Survey, using military personnel of the Royal Engineers accompanied by local people of knowledge (meresmen), undertook surveys in 1882-3. The initial reports were in the form of Boundary Report Books.

The present parish of Ilsington lies within the boundary shown. It is essentially an amalgamation of what were in the past the separate manors of Ilsington, Ingsdon, Bagtor, Sigford and Staplehill. These five manors are shown in the Exeter Domesday Book of 1086 as held by Ralph Pagnell (Ilsington and part of Ingsdon), Osbern of Sacey (also part of Ingsdon), Nicholas the Bowman, the one in charge of military operations involving the use of siege weapons (Bagtor and Staplehill), and Roald Dubbed, who held Sigford. A sixth early holding but not identified as a manor in 1086 was Horridge. Before the Conquest, Ralph Pagnell's manors were held by Merleswein, Osbern's by Frawin, Nicholas's by Ordric and Brictwald and Dubbed's by Brictric, presumably all Saxons.

The Conquest saw the whole of Devon placed under 52 landholders, compared with some eight times that number before. This amalgamation, together with the subsequent growth of early churches, may have helped define parish boundaries including that of Ilsington. Table 1 shows the principal entries in Exeter Domesday for the manors:

	Ilsington (Pagnell)	Ingsdon (Pagnell)	Ingsdon (Osbern)	Bagtor (Nicholas)	Sigford (Dubbed)	Staplehill (Nicholas)
Ploughs (actual)	8	7	6	5	½	½
Ploughs (potential)	12	9	6	5	1½	2
Villagers*	28	28	18	8	nil	7
Slaves	7	5	2	1	nil	nil
Value	£9	£9	40s.	20s.	5s.	5s.
Woodland	210	70	12	3	6	6
Pasture	2 leagues & 8 furlongs in both length and width	4	40	1 league long and ½ league wide		
Meadow	1	1	8	nil	nil	6

(All areas in acres unless otherwise shown. *Includes smallholders.)

It is not possible to state at all accurately the early division of Ilsington parish between the original manors within it. Reichel did much work in trying to calculate the likely areas of manors within Devonshire. His method was based on subtracting from the whole area of a parish, as shown for ecclesiastical purposes, ten per cent for 'road wastes, linches and mere balks'. Using the Domesday record he also deducted any specific areas given for meadow, wood and pasture. The remaining area was divided by the number of ploughs shown in Domesday. Ploughland was taken to be the amount which a full team of eight oxen could plough 'working at set times according to the custom of those days'. He arrived at values which varied somewhat from parish to parish but approximated to 100 acres per plough team. He also reasoned that the *leuca* or *lug*, translated generally as league, was a different dimension depending upon whether it referred to length or breadth. Commons and unallotted wastes were not included in the areas resulting from these calculations. Reichel's values were:

Within Teignbridge Hundred
   Lestintone (Ilsington) Ralph Pagenal, 1,731 acres
   Ainechesdon (Ingsdon) Ralph Pagenal, 975 acres
   Ainichesdone (another part of Ingsdon) Osbern de Salceid, 660 acres

Within Wonford Hundred
   Bagetore (Bagtor) Nicholas the Bowman, 463 acres
   Sigeford (Sigford) Roald Dubbed, 134 acres
   Stapelie (Staplehill) Nicholas the Bowman, 178 acres

Reichel also took the Domesday entry for Rocombe as being synonymous with that of Horridge in Ilsington parish and assigned to it an area of 251 acres, but was on very weak ground. Rocombe lies in Stokeinteignhead parish in a detached part of Wonford Hundred. It does not appear in later

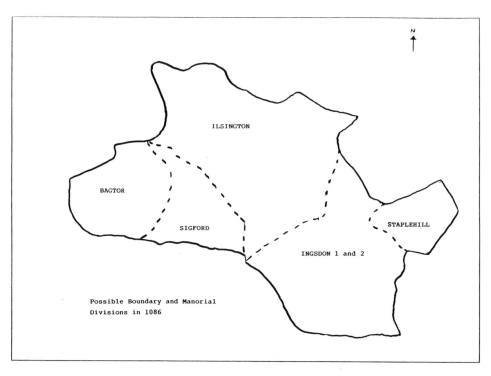

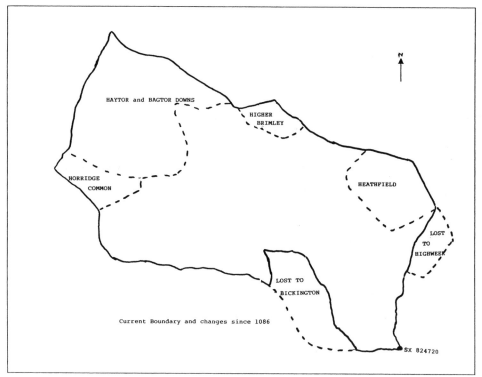

Fig. 3 *Map of the manorial boundaries in 1086 and today.*

fees lists whereas Haurig (Horridge) does and lies geographically in that part of Ilsington parish which also lay in Wonford Hundred. The probability is that Horridge was already included in the Domesday entry for Bagtor or became part of it later. Reichel also believed Lewendone in Domesday to be Liverton in Ilsington parish but it was almost certainly Lowton in Moretonhampstead parish.

The calculation of Domesday acreages are fraught with difficulty. In particular, dimensions given in leagues may, at times, merely give the extremes of length and width and should not be taken to imply a continuous area encompassed within them. The comments of Darby and Welldon Finn in relation to measurements should be noted: 'It is impossible to tell and we certainly cannot assume that a definite geometrical figure was in the minds of those who supplied the information. Nor can we hope to convert these measurements into modern acreages by an arithmetical process.'

While it is clear that the modern boundary of the civil parish of Ilsington and the area enclosed within it owed much to the extents of the manors shown, it is probable that the total area identified in Domesday was much smaller than that of today, which is 7,843 acres. Waste land was seldom identified or included and certainly was not shown specifically for the six manors. That waste would have embraced Haytor and Bagtor Downs which amount to some 1,700 acres. Horridge Common, too, of some 250 acres in extent may, as we have seen, been excluded as common land or included in the return for Bagtor. Heathfield is a name which meant waste land. An Enclosure Act of 1809 showed Ilsington Heathfield to be of 800 acres and this also was likely to have been ignored in Domesday.

The entries show land believed capable of being ploughed as well as the number of ploughs on the land. Thus Ilsington Manor had land for 12 ploughs but only 8 in existence: the two entries for Ingsdon showed 15 and 13 ploughs; Bagtor, 5 and 5 ploughs; Staplehill, 2 and half a plough, Sigford 1½ and half a plough. The entries show that Ilsington Manor and the two Ingsdons formed the bulk of the parish with ploughland in the latter being close to its expected potential. This may reflect the improved agricultural quality of the land in the southern and lower levels compared to that nearer to the moor. The bulk of the population, too, were in Ingsdon. The fact that no population figures were given for Sigford, although unusual, is not unique in Domesday entries. It may well be that labour was supplied from nearby Bagtor Manor, for land for only half a plough is recorded as being in use in Sigford.

From all the foregoing it is clear that the two Ingsdons together were close neighbours and somewhat larger than Ilsington Manor, and contained the most population, fertile land and livestock. The parish took its name, however, from the site of the early church. There is some evidence to suggest that the Ingsdon of Osbern was in the area known today as South Knighton. Thus the Tax Roll of Testa de Nevil (19-27 Henry III), as transcribed by Whale, shows the Earl of Devon holding in demesne one knight's fee in South Knighton and one fee in Ingsdon, alias Knighton Beaumont. The Ingsdon of Pagnell descended to the Beaumonts so it would seem highly probable that this was synonymous with Knighton Beaumont and the Ingsdon of Osbern de Sacey with South Knighton. It has not proved possible to follow the descent or line of the Ingsdon held in 1086 by Osbern de Sacey but it is conjectured that it may have extended into what is now the manor of Bickington, for it is known that an early landowner there (c.1150-9) was Hugh de Saceid, clearly of the same family as Osbern. (Neither Bickington nor any of the villages within it feature in Domesday, the earliest references being in the Charter Rolls for 1107 and the Assize Rolls for 1219.) It is suggested that the line of this Ingsdon may have followed the river Lemon to take in Ramshorn and Lurcombe, which lay on the boundary of Peadington, and continued until the river turned abruptly south at SX 824720 approximately. The current boundary between the parishes of Ilsington and Bickington turns sharply at Combe but this smacks more of an arrangement designed to accommodate the arrival of a new ecclesiastical boundary for Bickington in the 15th century than of a boundary definition of 1086.

The Domesday entry for Staplehill shows that it was substantially larger than Sigford and it is conjectured that it then comprised what later became known as Lower Staplehill in Ilsington parish and Higher Staplehill in Highweek. A prehistoric track, the Goatpath, ran from Great Haldon to Staverton passing through Ash Hill, with both Lower and Higher Staplehill to the west and Highweek to the east. It may have helped define boundaries in 1086. In earlier times the boundary of Ilsington to the north east was also somewhat different to what it is today. The manor of Langaller, not itself recognised in Domesday, fell within the manor of Bovey Tracey held in 1086 by the Bishop of Coutances. A holding of 'Bremley', now Brimley, was specifically mentioned in a court book of Langaller for 1602. By 1604 a Lower Brimley was recognised and by 1606 a Higher Brimley also, so in those years both the Brimleys were taken to be in Langaller. Disputes over the rightful position of Higher Brimley continued over the years, resulting in some confusion which found partial expression in an Abstract of Title to the lands of the Earl of Devon. An entry for Langaller states, 'All that the manor of Langaller with its appurtenances situate in the parishes, villages and fields of Bovey Tracey, Ilsington and Sigmore or one of them in the County of Devon'. It is clear that in 1086 Higher Brimley did not lie in Ilsington parish as it now does.

IV

THE MANORS

Ilsington

Ralph Pagnell, the lord of the manor of Ilsington in 1086, had a son Fulk who succeeded to his Devonshire estates but they passed, probably in the 12th century, to William Peverel and his sister Matilda. The Peverel estates escheated to the Crown in the reign of Henry II (1154-89), probably as a consequence of the support given by the Peverels to Stephen in his conflict with the Empress Matilda, for Henry was her son. The Ilsington manor then passed to the Beaumont family notably associated in early times with Shirwell in Shirwell Hundred. The first known documentary evidence for the association with Ilsington lies between 1235 and 1242 when Philip de Bello Monte held the manor for one knight's fee from the Honour of Plymthon (Plympton). Between 1284 and 1286 Feudal Aids shows Oliver Dynham as holding Ilsington and Ingsdon for one knight's fee from Richard Beaumont, Richard holding it from Isabella, Countess of Devon, and Isabella holding from the King, a good example of the hierarchical structure in those times. An Inquisition Post Mortem (IPM) on Oliver's death held at Bishops Clyst in 1299 shows that he then held the manor from Philip de Bello Monte, the son and heir of the Richard named above, who was born in 1271.

The tax roll for Devon in 1303 shows that a John de Beaumond and Isabella de Fishacre jointly held Ilsington Manor and Ingsdon. Whether Isabella was ever lady of the manor is uncertain but her relationship with the Dynhams was close for she had a daughter, Margaret, who married Joce de Dynham. Joce died around 1301 and left a son and heir, John, born in 1295. In 1316 Sir John de Vautort, giving evidence at an IPM to establish proof of John's age, stated that he saw John two days after his birth at Nutwell in the lap of Isabella (helping out no doubt in the time-honoured way of grandmothers). In 1332 an IPM on the death of John de Dynham shows that he held the manor from Hugh Courtenay with Isabel holding for life for 2d. yearly.

For a long time the Dynhams continued to hold Ilsington Manor. A John born in 1433 was the last male heir. Although married twice he left no legitimate male issue. He had three brothers who all died without issue and five sisters, one of whom, Edith, probably died also without issue before John's death in 1501. By then he was Lord Dynham and High Treasurer of

England. He was buried in the choir of Greyfriars Church in London which has long since vanished. His heirs were his four sisters, and they and their husbands are shown below:

> The eldest, Margaret, married Nicholas, Baron Carew and she and her husband were buried in Westminster Abbey. Their son and heir was Sir Edmund of Mohuns Ottery.
> Elizabeth, the next oldest, married Fulk Bourchier, Lord Fitzwarine, who died in 1479. Their son and heir John became the 1st Earl of Bath.
> Katherine, the third sister, married Sir Thomas Arundell, who died in 1485 and left a son and heir Sir John of Lanherne.
> Joan married John, Lord Zouche, who died in 1526.

With the death of Lord Dynham the first major dispersal of the manorial property began for (with no regard for the difficulties which would be met by future historians!) he left a quarter share of his Ilsington manors and many other properties to each of his sisters. The passage of these shares to the heirs in the later years of the 16th century is complex but there is good evidence that the Carew portion passed quickly to the Compton family of Compton Winyates for by 1548 an IPM on William Compton showed that he held, *inter alia*, one quarter part of Ilsington Manor. This part descended to Peter Compton and then to his son, Henry, for in 1566 a survey made of Peter's possessions showed that he owned a fourth part of the lands called 'the Lord Dynham's Lands in the counties of Devon and Cornwall'. While the Arundell portion then still remained with that family the Bath and Zouche portions were held by George Ford, the son of John Ford, a man with many holdings in Devon.

By 1609 a further quarter portion had passed to the Ford family for in his will dated 5 May in that year Thomas Ford, born in 1536 and the son and heir of George, conveyed to his wife Elizabeth 'all my three parts of the Manor of Ilsington together with the mansion house of Ilsington and all messuages and land thereunto belonging'. No explicit proof of a purchase by Thomas of this third portion has been found but there are gaps in the Calendar of Enrolled Deeds for Ilsington during the period 1536 to 1675. However, the third portion would have been that formerly held by the Comptons, for a survey undertaken in 1609 for John Arundell of Lanherne showed that family still possessed a quarter share of the manor of Ilsington. The grandson of Thomas and Elizabeth, Henry, became Sir Henry of Nutwell, MP for Tiverton and Secretary of State for Ireland. In 1651 he married Eleanour Row, daughter of Sir Henry Row. When Sir Henry Ford died in 1684 he was seriously in debt and had to leave the bulk of his estate to his devisees to pay the debts, funeral expenses and legacies to his four daughters. After such payments the barton of Bagtor was to go to his grandson and any part of the estate remaining to his son Charles. The provisions of the will caused much dissension which was only finally resolved some eight years later by an award of arbitration made in 1692. The awards of relevance to this history stated that John Drake, John Egerton and Edward Holwell were, *inter alia*, to be awarded equal parts of the high rent of Ilsington, Bagtor and Notsworthy. John Drake had married Sir Henry's daughter Catherine, John Egerton her sister Sarah and Edward Holwell their sister Elizabeth. Egerton also received half of Rora, an old demesne holding. There was no specific mention of the other demesne holding, namely the Court Barton of Ilsington. (These demesne holdings are dealt with later.)

The manor having been broken into four parts following the death of Lord Dynham, the three parts gathered together under the Ford family now became dispersed again. High rents were paid to the owners of the commons on the moor, their receipt being a prerogative of the lord of the manor, and here we have three recipients. Nevertheless, the lordship passed eventually to the descendants of John Egerton, although not before reference was made in an account book of the charity relating to William Candy to Egerton Filmore, Jane and Eleanour Holwell and Phillis Drake as lord and ladies of the manor.

John Egerton passed his portion of the manor to his son, John, Rector of East Allington, and in 1730 this John devised it to Egerton Filmore of Lympstone. Land Tax assessment records show that Egerton Filmore alone was assessed for three parts of the commons up until 1780 and so clearly had become the principal lord of the manor. Filmore left two daughters as co-heiresses, Sarah and Elizabeth, but Sarah soon died, being buried on 9 January 1789. Elizabeth continued to be the lady of the manor until her marriage in 1795 to John Searle, the marriage being witnessed by William Emlin Filmore. The lordship of the manor then passed to John Searle until his death in 1808. His widow survived him by only a year and in her will she left her cousin Emlin Filmore the manors of Ilsington, Bagtor and Notsworthy. Other properties within Ilsington parish were left to her cousin Abraham Filmore.

The fourth part of the manor, as already stated, was owned by the Arundell family at least up to 1609. By 1780 this fourth part was owned by James Templer, who may have acquired it at any time after 1609 but no records have been found to show just when. James was the founder of the family fortune, also owning the manor of Teigngrace and building the new Stover House completed in 1780. He was succeeded by his son, also named James, born in 1748. James married Mary, daughter of James Buller of Morval, and died in 1813. He was succeeded by his son George. By 1819 George Templer was possessed of the whole manor having, presumably, purchased the remainder from Emlin Filmore. By Michaelmas 1829 the lordship had passed from George Templer to Edward Adolphus, 11th Duke of Somerset, born Lord Seamore in 1775 and becoming duke in 1793 following the death of his father. Edward Adolphus died in 1855 to be succeeded by his son, also Edward Adolphus, the 12th Duke, who died without male issue in 1885.

By 1888 the lordship had passed to R.R. Wolfe, who in that year also acquired the Leighon estate which lay just outside the Ilsington boundary in the neighbouring parish of Manaton. Wolfe was a prebendary of Exeter Cathedral who had previously been Rector of Upton, Torquay. He died in 1902 and the whole estate was put on the market. It was acquired at auction by Washington Merrit Grant Singer, the second son of the Singer of sewing machine fame. Singer was a wealthy man with other properties in London, Salisbury, Newmarket and Paignton. He was a racehorse owner and also Master of the South Devon Hunt. When Singer died in 1934 he was succeeded by his second wife, Ellen Mary, who, with John Edward Eastley, solicitor, was executor of the Leighon estate and in that capacity they were jointly lady and lord of the manor. In 1944 the estate was purchased by John Crocker Bulteel. In 1964 the Leighon estate was sold in nine lots, lot eight including over 1,000 acres of Haytor Down and lot nine being the title to the lordship of the manors of Ilsington and Bagtor, now separated from land ownership and specifically described as one of courtesy only. Haytor Down and the title went to Robert Cyril Longsdon, a stepson of Singer. When Longsdon put the estate up for sale in 1975 the title did not sell, but Devon County Council bought most of Haytor Down. Longsdon continued to hold the title until 1978 when it was bought by Antony and Audrey Cullen of Leighon House, Manaton. In 1997 the ownership of Haytor Down was transferred to the Dartmoor National Park.

Ingsdon

As already shown, Ralph Pagnell held the manors of both Ilsington and Ingsdon in 1086 and Osbern held another part of Ingsdon. The descent of Osbern's part is not known although there is reason to postulate that it might have been absorbed in the neighbouring parish of Bickington. Pagnell's holdings passed, as we have noted, to the Peverels and then to the Beaumonts. By 1228 a William Beaumont held Ingsdon from Phillip Beaumont and by 1284 Richard Beaumont held it from the Countess of Devon with Oliver Dynham as tenant. In 1303 John Beaumont and Isabella de Fishacre held it jointly and in 1325/6 a dispute between a William Barry and John Beaumont resulted in William granting the manor to John to hold for life.

After John's death Pagnell's Ingsdon passed to his son Matthew and then to Matthew's heirs. About twenty years later John Dynham and John Beaumont held it jointly. In 1377 an IPM on Hugh de Courtenay showed that Ingsdon was held by a John Beaumont, quite possibly that same John but the name was an extremely common one in those days. By 1428 the manor seems to have been held by William Beaumont, Yvo Horege, John Copplestone and John Stapelhyll. An IPM held at Exeter on 29 October 1471 showed that 'John Beaumont held … in his demesne as of fee the manor of Enkedon [Ingsdon] worth by the year clear £10 held of Philip Beaumond'.

John's heir was his daughter Elizabeth, aged 19, who married Robert Pomeroy and in so doing brought the estate to that notable and wealthy family whose founder in England had been Ralph Pomeroy. He had accompanied the Conqueror and as reward for his support received 57 manors in Devon (and two more in Somerset). The richest of these was Berry Pomeroy. Some two centuries of Pomeroy ownership of Ingsdon followed this marriage and several family members were buried at Ilsington: Hugh on 3 March 1602, his son Thomas on 25 April 1610, Richard in 1616 and Thomas in 1662. Thomas's son, also named Thomas, sold Ingsdon to John Stowell some five months after the death of his father.

In the neighbouring parish of Bovey Tracey there is a monument in the parish church to Sir John Stowell. It records that he died on 19 January 1669 aged forty-four. Somewhere around 1672 the devisees of his estate sold Ingsdon to James Rodd of Bedford House, Exeter. When Rodd died he left a will which bequeathed, 'All that ye reversion of the barton of Ingsdon, also Ingsdon & Penwood in the parish of Ilsington ... to my son Bampfylde during his life and then to his two sons James and Joseph respectively.'

Ingsdon was acquired sometime before 1699 by John Battishill of South Tawton. John married Elizabeth Pinsent of Woodland, who was herself the sole issue of a marriage between Thomas Pinsent and Joan Berry of Halwell. John and Elizabeth are shown in the Woodland parish register as married on 24 June 1672 and they had a son and heir of forename Pinsent baptised on 24 January 1681 as well as four daughters, Elizabeth, Honor, Jane and Agnes. Pinsent Battishill was buried at Ilsington on 19 March 1707 and held Ingsdon for only six years after his father died in 1699. Elizabeth, Jane and Agnes became joint heiresses, their mother and sister Honor dying in 1705 and 1707 respectively. Both Jane and Agnes died without legitimate issue leaving Elizabeth as sole heir.

Elizabeth married Robert Tapson and although the date and place of this has not been determined there is ample evidence for it contained within an indenture of 1743 which mentions 'Robert Tapson of Ingsdon and John Tapson of the same place, eldest son and heir at law of the said Robert Tapson by Elizabeth his late deceased wife who was one of the four sisters and coheiresses of Pinsent Battishill late of Ingsdon deceased ...'. Robert and Elizabeth had four children baptised at Ilsington and the second son, also named Robert, succeeded his father to the estate. Robert Tapson junior died on 11 July 1750 and in his will left to George Fursdon, *inter alia*, 'all that my mannors and lordships or reputed mannors or lordship and barton or farm of or called Ingsdon in the said County of Devon'. There seems to have been no family relationship between Tapson and Fursdon, just a close friendship. Tapson's heir at law was an aunt Elizabeth Tapson of Tavistock and she, at Robert's request, confirmed the validity of the will.

George Fursdon was of Fursdon Lacey in the parish of Cadbury. He became High Sheriff and Deputy Lieutenant of Devon and in 1753 married Elizabeth

Cheyney. She died whilst still young and George married again, this time Grace Sydenham of Coombe, the daughter of Humphrey Sydenham who was MP for Exeter. George was buried at Cadbury on 11 November 1772 and Grace on 3 July 1780. George Sydenham Fursdon was born in 1771 and was clearly not of age when his father died. However, it seems that Ingsdon had passed from the Fursdon family before then for a conveyance of 1766, not directly concerned with Ingsdon, refers to 'Charles Hale of Ingsdon'.

Hale and Fursdon do not seem to have been directly related to one another but were just good friends. Charles' father was Charles Hale, a Londoner who married Martha Samber at Westminster in 1720. Charles junior married Anne Carpenter at Launceston in 1754 and they had no children. When he died in 1795 he left to Anne, his friends Hugh Ackland and the Reverend Nutcombe, Chancellor of the Cathedral of Exeter, the capital messuage, barton and demesne lands of Ingsdon to be used for the benefit of Anne during her lifetime (as well as many other properties in neighbouring parishes). At his request Charles was buried at Cadbury. Upon her death, which occurred in 1805, the life interest went to his kinsman, James Samber, Captain in the Royal Navy. James Samber died in 1821 and the estate was then passed to the heirs of his daughter, Martha, she having predeceased him. Martha had married James Monro in 1805 and their son and heir, with forenames Charles Hale, succeeded to the estates. He was only seven years old on his mother's death and John Pidsley of Exeter was the receiver appointed by Chancery to act for Charles during his minority. Ingsdon manor house and the adjoining lands were leased, through John Pidsley in 1821, to Hugh Dyke Acland for seven years.

The Monros were a branch of the ancient Scottish house of Monro of Fowlis. The Scottish connection continued with the marriage at York in 1827 of Charles Hale Monro to Mary Jane, daughter of Patrick Macdougall of Dunolly, Argyllshire. Mary died in 1858 and Charles was married again in 1860, this time to Ann Spooner, eldest surviving daughter of William Bowie of Bath.

Charles Hale Monro died at Ingsdon in 1867 and two years later the manor house was rebuilt, presumably at the direction of the heir, Charles James Hale Monro, born in 1829. He became a Captain in the 36th Foot Regiment and continued as the owner of the manor until 1902 when it was sold to the Filles du Esprit of St Brieuc (known as the White Sisters). Other parts of the estate passed to E.H. Bayldon, Deputy Lieutenant of Devon and also a JP of Dawlish. Bayldon is shown in *Kelly's Directory* of Devon for 1906 as a principal landowner in Ilsington parish but not as a resident. No mention is made of him in the *Directory* for 1914.

In 1972 the convent closed and became a school for 'educationally challenged' boys. This may not have been a good move for in 1977 it was damaged by fire to such an extent that it never re-opened. In 1985 the fire-damaged buildings were sold by auction at the *Globe Hotel*, Newton Abbot together with 12 acres of land. Much of it was purchased by a property developer and the site of the old manor house has now suffered the ultimate fate and become executive-style houses.

Bagtor

The first documentary evidence of ownership after Domesday is an entry in the Testa de Nevil for the period 1235-43 which shows that William of Bagtor held it for one knight's fee: Feudal Aids for 1284-6 show that Thomas of Bagtor held it from Robert son of Pagan (clearly a descendant of Ralph Pagenal). In 1304 a Thomas held Bagtor and a William of Bagtor held half a fee in Horridge. By 1332 the Lay Subsidy Roll show Geoffrey of Bagtor taxed for 2s. and in 1346 Feudal Aids show Geoffrey paying 40s. for Bagtor and also refer to the fact that Thomas once held it

By 1377, however, there is a change of ownership, for William de Brightleigh held it for one knight's fee from Hugh de Courtenay. There is then a gap of some fifty years in our knowledge of ownership until in 1428 a John Ford had succeeded together with John Windyeat: 'Johnannes Forde et Johannes Windyeat tenet di f.m. in Bagetor quod Galfidus de Bagetor quondam tenuit ibidem' (John Ford and John Windyeat hold half a knight's fee in Bagtor which Geoffrey of Bagtor once held). There is an implication here, though not a certainty, that Ford and Windyeat were the immediate successors to Geoffrey. There is then a further unfortunate gap in knowledge for nearly a century and it is not until 1517 that we hear of a John Ford having purchased Bagtor from John Beare. Quite when, and for how long, the Beares owned Bagtor is not certain but there is a statement from Pole that a William Hurst, alderman of the city of Exeter, married Julian, daughter of Beare of Bagtor, and that the marriage took place around 1507. John Ford, the purchaser in 1517, was born about 1485 for he had a daughter, Joan, born in 1509. John was a leading figure in Ashburton and had amassed many estates in Devon. His heir was George, born in 1522, who was bequeathed some sixty per cent of his father's estates. George, however, was forced to sell much of this to pay for a dowry for the marriage of his sister, Margaret, John having made a manifestly insufficient allowance for this in his will. Bagtor, though, with other properties in Ilsington parish, was passed on George's death to his eldest son Thomas, born in 1556.

Thomas, by his wife Elizabeth Popham, had an heir, Henry of Bagtor (and a second son John, baptised at St Michael's Church, Ilsington, who became famous as an Elizabethan dramatist). Henry married Katherine Drake, daughter of George Drake of Littleham, in October 1612. In that same year he conveyed Bagtor to John Drake and John Sampson. Only four years later, however, Edward Gee, of Tedburn St Mary, John Drake and John Sampson sold to:

> Kathren, widdow of Henry Forde of Bagtor, esq., the lordshippe and manor of all Bagtorre with howses, milles, gardens, landes, pastures, woodes, marshes,

commons, waters etc, the capitall mansion howse, barton, farme and demesne landes of Bagtorre or so called ...

Henry and Katherine had a son and heir who became Sir Henry of Nutwell, whose disputed estates have already been mentioned in the section which dealt with the manor of Ilsington. From then until the present day the passage of this lordship followed the same route as that for Ilsington Manor.

Sir Henry specifically devised the barton of Bagtor to his grandson Henry, whose father was Henry Row Ford and who is most probably the boy shown in the Ilsington parish register as born on 20 November 1645. The ownership of Bagtor in the times of Sir Henry Ford, Henry Row Ford and the grandson Henry was complex and the legal issues generated finally found their way to the House of Lords (no doubt diminishing the wealth of the Ford family still more!). For a time it would seem that it belonged to a Sir Thomas Row of Swarford, Oxfordshire:

> The late Henry Row Ford, Sir Henry's son and heir, having purchased of Sir Thomas Row, Knt., late of Swarford, co. Oxon, and one Abraham Johnson his trustee, the Barton of Baytor [sic] co. Devon, worth about 100l a year, mortgaged it in CarlI 1, to Sir Thos. Row for £493 14s., part of the purchase money which he and his father covenanted to pay. The father paid about 622l on his son's account but, the son having neglected to pay the rest, Sir Thomas entered in 1673, but died in the lifetime of the mortgagors.

Sir Thomas Row was eventually paid the covenanted purchase price by the devisees and the barton became the property of the grandson of Sir Henry. This Henry Ford, the grandson, was described as a merchant of London and he was active in mortgaging the barton of Bagtor and other associated properties. In 1704 he conveyed the barton to Sir Henry Lear of Lindridge and John Lear of Shiphay but the Lears held for only a short while, for it was conveyed to Thomas Tothill of Bovey Tracey in 1707.

The Tothills were an Ideford family. Thomas married Elizabeth Drake, the daughter of Sir Bernard Drake of Bickington and Elizabeth Prestwood of Butterford, in 1701. He was succeeded by his son, also named Thomas, who was born in 1718 and became Vicar of Uplyme. He married Penelope Hill of Lydcott, Morval, Cornwall and after his death the properties passed to Penelope. She rented much of Bagtor to a Jonathan Bussell of Ilsington during her lifetime and on her death the properties passed to her heir, Penelope Elizabeth Tothill, baptised in 1747. When 21 years of age Penelope Elizabeth married Thomas Lane of Yealmpton; she died when aged fifty-six. Thomas disposed of Bagtor within four years of her death having acquired it, one supposes, through this marriage. Thomas, then of Newton Bushel, conveyed it to John Dunning.

John Dunning was born at Ashburton in 1731 and by all accounts was a most gifted boy. He followed in his father's footsteps in the legal profession and at an early age was taken under the wing of Sir Thomas Clarke, Master of the Rolls. John was entered as a student at the Middle Temple at the age of 21 and became an eminent lawyer and politician. He was most prominent in the latter capacity in debates in the House of Commons relating to the American war. His motion 'That it is the opinion of this committee that the influence of the Crown has increased, is increasing and ought to be diminished' was carried and found its way into textbooks as 'Dunning's Resolution'. He became Baron Ashburton in 1782 and also Chancellor of the Duchy of Lancaster. In 1780 he married Elizabeth Baring, whose two brothers founded the famous bank of that name. On his death in 1783 the title, together with a substantial fortune, passed to Richard Barre Dunning who was but some fifteen months old. In 1805 Richard married Anne, daughter of William Cunningham, which marriage allied him to the Cranstoun family for William had married one of the granddaughters of the 5th Baron Cranstoun. When Richard Barre Dunning died in 1823 he was without issue and his widow succeeded to the ownership of Bagtor during her lifetime, but following her death in 1835 the estate passed to James Edward, 10th Baron Cranstoun. *White's Directory* for Devon for 1850 reads, 'Lord Cranstoun of Scotland owns Bagtor where he occasionally resides in the old manor house formerly the seat of the Beares and Fords'. James Edward continued as owner until his death on 28 September 1869.

In that year it is believed that the rather shadowy figure of Margaret Macleod acquired the estate. She is likely to have been a Scottish relation of Richard Barre Dunning for she was referred to in his will. She had married the Baron de Virte, believed to be Italian, and afterwards was known as the Baroness Virte de Rathsawhawson. The first specific mention of her ownership of Bagtor is in *Kelly's Directory* for 1883 and she continues so to be designated until her death in 1904. She was then aged sixty-seven.

In 1935 the estate was put on the market together with other properties by the personal representatives of Alice Louisa Wilson. The Bagtor portion amounted to some 792 acres which included Bagtor House, Bagtor Barton, Bagtor Cottages, Bagtor Mill, Millcombe Cottages, Smith's Wood Cottage and a holding at Emsworthy. Mrs Wilson was the widow of Arthur Henry Wilson, a son of John Wilson who had married Anna Maria Isabella Macleod in Florence in 1846. Almost certainly John, and thus Arthur, would have been related through this marriage to the Baroness. It is believed that Arthur succeeded to the Bagtor estate shortly after her death.

The estate was sold to William Whitley who owned much adjoining land. In 1958 Whitley put the estate on the market and in the following year Bagtor House was sold with seven acres of land to John Perrin and occupied for some years by his mother who did much to renovate the property, which had suffered some neglect. It was sold in 1996 to Mr and Mrs Sawrey-Cookson who now reside there and have continued the renovation. Bagtor Barton was not sold until the 1960s to Harold Retallick, who had previously been a tenant. It is still in the ownership of the Retallick family.

Staplehill

It has already been suggested in Chapter III that Staplehill may have comprised at one time what later became known as Lower Staplehill in Ilsington parish and Higher Staplehill in Highweek parish. Documentary evidence of its descent is sparse. The earliest reference found dates from 1241 when Roger de Staplehill held it. By 1285 it was held (together with Stokeinteignhead) by Robert the son of Pagenal, almost certainly a descendant of Ralph Pagenal, the lord of the manors of both Ilsington and Ingsdon in 1086. It is also most likely that the heirs of Roger de Staplehill were actually in possession with Robert as their overlord. Somewhere between 1285 and 1303 a John de Staplehill was in possession for on the latter date Emma de Staplehill and her sisters, who were stated to be the heirs of John, held it. In 1346 a Richard Monson and John de Staplehill held Staplehill for half a knight's fee from the capital manor of Stokeinteignhead: 'De Ricardo Monson et Johanna de Staplehull pro di f.m. in Staplehull tento de Stoke in Tonhide i.c. quod Emma Staplehull cum soribus suis quondam tenuit.'

In 1377 the manor was held by William de Brightelegh and some fifty years later by John Staplehill, Geoffrey Polyng and Geoffrey Daran. Thereafter no documentary evidence has been found which can point specifically to

6 *Bagtor House, 2005. Photo courtesy of Mr and Mrs Sawrey-Cookson.*

this being a manor in its own right. Lord Clifford of Chudleigh owned Lower Staplehill from at least 1780 until 1810, when the owner became James Templer succeeded in 1827 by James's son George. Some three years later Lord Seamore became the owner. It has already been shown that the Templers and Lord Seamore were successively the lords of the manor of Ilsington and it is conjectured that some time between 1428 and 1780 any matters relating to the lands comprising Staplehill and its owners would have been dealt with by the Ilsington Manor Court.

Sigford

The earliest reference found after the Conquest is for 1284 when a Joel of Bukyngton (Bickington) held it from Robert Dynham, who held it himself from the Countess of Devon. A Joel was still holding in 1303. By 1341 John Daumarle held it for a quarter of a knight's fee from the castle of Plympton.

By 1346 we learn that, 'Joel de Bukyngton pro quarti parte un f.m. in Sigford tenta de Plympton i.c. quam Andreas de Trelesk quondam tenuit.' (Joel of Bickington for a quarter of a knight's fee in Sigford held of the Honour of Plympton in chief which Andrew of Trelesk once held.) Just when Andrew possessed Sigford has not been established but probably it was after 1284. Changes in ownership became common for in 1355 Joel of Bickington held it from John Daumarle; in 1392 John Daumarle was still holding, but by 1428 John Copylston and Henry Merwode held between them, but separately, a quarter of a knight's fee there. In 1493 Ralph Coplestone held Sigford 'by fealty only' from the Bishop of Exeter and in 1550 the Coplestones still held it from the Bishop. It was still an identifiable manor by 1563 when a bargain and sale was made by Christopher Coplestone to Robert Hayman of Newton Abbot of the 'two manners or lordeschippes called Sigfforde and Lovelane'. Fourteen years later a John Hayman sold these manors to his brother Nicholas. Nothing further has been found which specifically refers to Sigford as a manor.

In the 16th century George Ford was active in land transactions in Ilsington parish and its neighbours and it is possible, though conjectural, that George or his heirs purchased Sigford. By 1818 the court rolls for the manors of Bagtor and Ilsington show William Ball, Grace Layman and John Eales of Lower Sigford and John Ackland of Oxenham's Sigford in the list of commoners attending the court. It seems clear that by then Sigford had been included in the manor of Bagtor.

V

THE BARTON AND DEMESNE LANDS

The Court Barton

Barton and demesne lands were those over which only the lord or lady of the manor had proprietary rights but which were usually cultivated for the lord by his dependent tenants. The court barton consisted often of the manor house occupied by the lord together with adjacent lands contributing towards his income. However, both house and lands could be leased out in return for services and rents and the services, in time, were frequently waived in return for a payment. Leasing conveyed no more than the use and enjoyment of the land for a period of time; from the 15th century in Devon this was three lives, those of the tenant and two others nominated by him, commonly his wife and eldest son.

The first known reference to the barton and demesne lands of Ilsington is contained in a lease dated 20 November 1543 granted by Joan Arundell to Joan Ford and her son John Seyntclere. The lease was granted for a term of sixty years at an annual rent of 35s. 4d. It ceased on the death of either lessee but the the survivor would inherit following a payment of 3s. 4d. The lease required the upkeep of buildings, fences and ditches and in this connection rights of firebote, foldbote, ploughbote and geatbote were granted, that is the right to take wood for burning, maintenance of sheepfolds, making and repairing of gates and similar work. (The wording of the lease also implies that Joan Ford and William Bradleigh had possession before as lessees of Arundell.) Joan was the daughter of William Throwbridge and the widow of Gilbert Seyntclere, who died in 1526. Joan was re-married, this time to John Ford the Ashburton attorney, the father of George mentioned in the preceeding chapter as part owner of the Ilsington estates. (John Seyntclere, the joint lessee, had married a daughter of John Ford by the latter's first marriage.)

In 1566 the survey carried out by Henry Compton to establish the extent of his holdings had one section dealing specifically with barton and demesne lands and it is there that we learn for the first time the extent and nature of court barton:

> John Bolle held without indenture at will 1 granary house and bakehouse in Ilsington with 3 gardens, 1 acre; contains 1 close Wester Bowhill, 8 acres;

contains 1 close Easter Bowhill 6 acres; contains 1 close Basheley 10 acres; contains 1 close Boysley mede 3½ acres; contains 1 close Lanepark 2 acres; contains 1 close Furze park cleves with moor and aldergrove 20 acres; contains 1 close the Beare and Newe close 3 acres; contains 1 close of wood called Northe Wood where is growing oak and other wood 30 acres; 1 meadow 1 acre; 1 little close Chenyshays 2 acres; and pays 35s. 4d.

The total area of barton lands under this section totals to 86½ acres. In another section, also stated to be barton lands, was a close called Cowdowne close 'now called Bowdens Park now lying in three parts which contain in all 25 acres'. This was held by John Bowden, and additionally Gabriel Wyger held two closes of barton land totalling 35 acres.

Despite the lease for sixty years, clearly neither Joan Ford nor John Seyntclere had continued until 1566 as lessees. It is likely that the barton land leased by Joan Arundell in 1543 was broadly the same as that held by John Bolle for the rents paid were the same, namely 35s. 4d. Little else is known of John Bolle; his wife Elizabeth was buried at Ilsington in 1574 and John himself in 1578. In the 1566 survey the manor house is shown separately from the holding of John Bolle: 'George Fourd esquire holds the capital mansion or house called the Manor Place of Ilsington with all house buildings gardens and orchards belonging to the same and pays per annum 2s. 8d.'

A survey roll of the lands of John Arundell of Lanherne in 1609 itemised the quarter part of the manor belonging to his son. Thomas Ford, Elizabeth his wife and Henry their son were shown as tenants of 'the capitall messuage 30 acres' for which they paid 8s. 10d. (again equal to 35s. 4d. for the whole). Thomas in his will conveyed all his three parts of the manor together with the manor house to his wife.

We have seen in the preceding chapter something of the problems besetting the estate of Sir Henry Ford (the grandson of Thomas), culminating in the arbitration award. This made no specific reference to the court barton and we must assume it was sold to help pay the debts or possibly passed to his son Charles, the residuary legatee. We next hear of it in the Ilsington parish register for 22 September 1726 when Philip Nanson is stated to be the owner. Nanson was the vicar of St Michael's church (and as we shall see later a firm believer in extracting all the vicarial dues from the parishioners). Nanson's daughter Catherine, it is believed, acquired court barton and sold it to a Mr Cock of whom we know nothing for certain, but a Thomas Cock owned Liverton mills by 1780.

In 1755 we have the first known account of the manor house by Jeremiah Milles:

> Next adjoining to the church on ye east side is ye Barton of Court. The house shows some signs of ancient grandeur. In one of the kitchen windows I observed the following coat of arms: In a border engrailed, party per fesse argent and sable, a greyhound running in chief, and an owl on base, counter-charged impaled with argent. Three bulls heads sable charged with a crescent.

These last are the arms of Waldron ... The same coat in another window with party pr. pale or at a star of six points countercharged.

The description of the principal arms corresponds with those granted to John Ford of Ashburton in 1524. The Waldron arms were no doubt incorporated

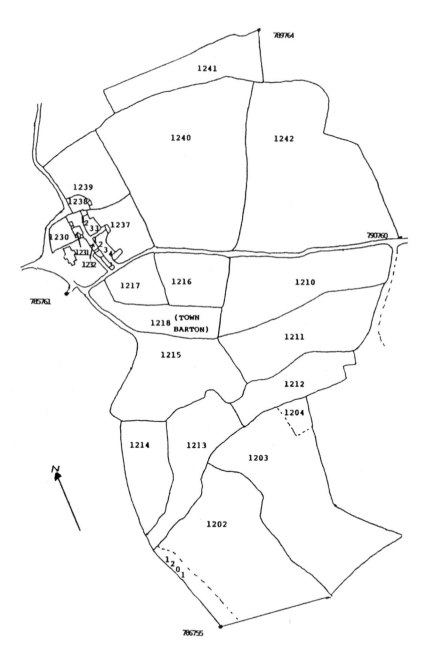

Fig. 4 *Map of the fields forming the court barton estate in 1838.*

by reason of Waldron's daughter becoming the third wife of John Ford and the mother of George. In 1777 court barton was advertised to let for 14 years and comprised the mansion house, barns, stables and other outhouses, gardens and 63 acres of arable meadow and pasture with rights of common on Haytor Down. It was probably let to James Mudge for three years later Charles Hale is shown as the owner and Mudge as tenant. Hale and Mudge continued as owner and tenant until 1795 when Hale's widow, Ann, becomes the owner and Robert Petherbridge tenant. The ownership passed down to the heirs of Hale in the way that the manor of Ingsdon did. Thus James Samber continued as owner from 1805 to 1821 with, from 1809, Charles Wills as occupier. In 1822 Charles Hale Monro was owner and not long afterwards there is evidence that the manor house had deteriorated, an account stating:

> The manor or Court Barton is close to the Church and was the residence of the Dinhams. The present house is dilapidated, is Elizabethan and was originally in the shape of an E. The end buildings remain but the intermediate range has gone. The granite arched entrance is perfect. In the 17th century a branch of the Ford family resided here and painted glass with their arms is in the hall ...

By 1829 Charles Hale Monro was part owner together with William Northway. Northway's part ownership would have occurred through his purchase of the court barton farmhouse which was probably adjacent to the manor house (and is now the *Carpenter's Arms*). Quite when the manor house became uninhabitable is not certain but in 1811 the Southwards occupied it, Sam Southward being born there that year. Clearly by 1852 it was empty, an article in the *Exeter Flying Post* referring to 'The remains of a mouldering mansion house, once vast and venerable ... '.

Charles Hale Monro was succeeded by his son and heir Charles James Hale Monro in 1867. An indenture of 1871 shows that Charles James conveyed to the vicar Robert Lovett and the churchwardens John Hill Clark and George Reeves a piece of the court barton estate adjacent to the old manor house, by then in near total ruin. This was to provide land for the building of Ilsington School (of which more later). Thus passed away the bulk of the ruined manor house although vestiges still remain, including an ivy-covered wall in the north-eastern corner of the churchyard with an overmantel and some carved stones. Around the parish, hedges and walls still have pieces of granite mullions and lintels 'borrowed' from the ruins in the time-honoured way of rural expediency.

In 1838 an agreement for the commutation of tithes necessitated the making of a survey and a schedule to determine the payment to which individuals were liable. The survey took the form of a map which was the earliest detailed map of the parish. It was at a scale of 1:2500 and numbered each piece of land. The entry for the court barton estate is shown below.

Field No.	Name	Type of Land	Size acres	roods	poles
1201	Church Lake	W	0	3	10
1202	Church Lake	A	7	3	6
1203	Newtake	A	9	2	29
1204	Newtake	W	0	2	0
1210	Higher Basley	A	5	0	8
1211	Lower Basley	A	4	0	32
1212	Lower Court Moor	P	2	0	11
1213	Higher Court Moor	P	3	1	18
1214	Lamb Park	A	2	2	30
1215	Basley Meadow	P	5	0	10
1216	Drew Meadow	P	2	0	27
1217	Court Orchard	O	1	0	2
1230	Church Yard Orchard	O	0	1	16
1231	Garden	G	0	0	8
1232	Plot	A	0	0	15
1233	Garden	G	0	0	24
1234	Barn, Linhay & Yard	Buildings	0	1	16
1237	New Orchard	O	1	1	0
1238	Cottage & Garden	Cottage etc.	0	0	23
1239	New Close	A	2	0	38
1240	Broom Park	A	11	1	20
1241	Stray Park	A	3	0	20
1242	Riddle Field	A	11	2	4
		Total	**75**	**0**	**7**

A (Arable), G (Garden), O (Orchard), P (Pasture), W (Waste)
(40 poles are equal to one rood and 4 roods to one acre.)

There are some similarities between the names and sizes of fields in the 1566 survey and the tithe map. Basheley and Boysley of the former probably equate to Higher and Lower Basley and Basley Meadow, Lane Park to Lamb Park and Newe Close to New Close. Northe wood is now known as Ilsington wood. In 272 years changes are to be expected, however, and a close comparison is not feasible. The areas, too, have changed from 121 acres to 105 acres (including Ilsington wood).

Rora

Rora is also shown in the 1566 survey as being demesne land. The first known reference to Rora, however, is in a Pipe Roll of 14 Henry III (1230) where one Richard owes half a mark for a pledge. The name is believed to derive from the word 'ore' or 'ora' meaning 'a boundary' and it is suggested that the boundary in question may have been that of Peadington portrayed in Chapter III. Indeed, the interpretation of the line of that boundary has been based in part on the position of Rora.

In 1494 an indenture was made between John, Lord Dynham and Joan Northway, the translation of which reads:

> Let all present and those in the future know that I John Dynham, Lord of Dynham, knight have given conceded and by this my present indentured charter confirmed to Joan Northway and to John her son and Joan his wife and John the son of those same John and Joan all my messuage lands and tenements with appurtenances at Le Rore in my manor of Ilsington which the said Joan Northway held the same earlier to have and to hold all the aforesaid … to the aforesaid Joan and John her son and Joan his wife and John the son of those same John and Joan for the term of their life and of the one of them shall live the longest.

We see from this that Joan Northway had held Rora before that date. The indenture goes on to show that the rent was to be 40s. a year and the tenants were to pay suit at the court of Lord Dynham and that of his heirs twice a year. As with court barton, there were rights of haybote, firebote and foldbote. One of the witnesses to the indenture was a Thomas Hexte whose name appears later in this account of the demesne land. The lease was granted for three lives, a further example of the practice which probably arose in Devon in the latter part of the 15th century.

The next known document referring explicitly to Rora as a demesne land occurs in the 1566 survey already referred to. Given below is a translation of the entry:

> John Northway holds for the term of his life given under the seal of John Dynham, Lord Dynham on the morrow of All Saints in the 10th year of Henry VII all messuages, lands and holdings with appurtenances at Lez Rora in the manor of Ilsington and there belongs to the said holdings 1 dwelling house in which he lives and another farmhouse; 1 orchard; 1 garden ½ acre; close Culver parke 4 acres; close New parke 3 acres; close the Wood parke 3 acres; close Higher Lange land 2½ acres; close Lower Lange land 3 acres; close Buttor 5 acres; close Gillhill parke 4 acres; close the Manno parke 4 acres; 2 closes Higher Marshes lying together 6 acres; close Lower Marshe 6 acres; close the Mede next the Garden 1 acres; meadow close Longemede 2 acres; 1 small meadow ½ acre; close Little parke ½ acre; waste Bower downe and the wood in which is growing oak etc., containing in all, with 20 acres of wood, 40 acres and pays per annum with suit 40s. 0d.

The entry refers at the beginning to the 1494 indenture and the rental remains the same. In the margin of the document and in another hand is the entry 'Reversion granted to Alexander his son and to Richard son of the said Alexander and Agnes wife of the said Richard for a term of 90 years by indenture if they so long live for a fine of £29.' Rora is written in the plural in the 1566 survey but in the singular in the indenture of 1494 and it had, indeed, become divided in the intervening period.

In a deed of 1568 George Ford is shown as owning, *inter alia*, half of 'Roner or Ronara' and half a dovehouse belonging to it but in the tenure of

John Northway and Alexander Northway. In 1593 another lease was effected between John Arundell and his wife Anne and John Northway, yeoman of Ilsington. The Arundells leased their portion of Rora, stated to be one quarter of the whole, for a term of 90 years and again on three lives, those of John and his son and daughter, Thomas and Margaret, if they should live so long. The rent was to be 10s. a year, one quarter of the earlier rental but accurately reflecting the quarter ownership then of the Arundells. The lease referred to a dovecot and to Rora wood as well as containing more general references to gardens, orchards, moors and commons. In 1609 a survey roll of the lands held in Devon by John Arundell showed that John Northway, aged 45, held a quarter part of Rora with his son Thomas and his daughter Margaret. Heriot was shown as a quarter of a best beast or 16s. in lieu thereof.

On 28 November 1622 Johan Northway, daughter of John and baptised in 1601, married William Bickford. This was the introduction of Bickford to Rora for a child, baptised in 1623 is shown in the parish registers as the son of William Bickford 'de Rowra'. In 1630 a church rate list shows that John Northway was paying 3s. 4d. and Thomas Northway and William Bickford 12d. each. Clearly John had the major part of Rora. The last specific mention of a Northway being associated with Rora was in 1663. Recorded data found after that is fragmentary but an indenture of 1722 mentions an assignment to Sampson Hele, his wife Elizabeth and Thomas Baker of 'all that moiety of one undivided messuage and tenement with the appurtenances in Rora and one dovehouse and all that wood commonly called Rora Wood'.

In Chapter IV the passage of Ilsington Manor down to Elizabeth Filmore was followed and she appears in Land Tax assessment records as being both occupier and owner of Rora in 1790. In her will of 1808 she devised Rora Farm to her cousin Abraham Filmore and Rora Wood to Emlin Filmore. Abraham continued as owner until 1838 when he was succeeded by his son Lewis of Stoke Damarel. In 1838 the schedule accompanying the tithe map of the parish shows Lewis as the owner of 191 acres and 34 perches of Rora Farm with John Mortimore as the occupier. In 1829 Emlin Filmore mortgaged Rora Wood to Sibella Hext and James Hext of Staverton but the conveyance gave Emlin the right to repay the sum she must have borrowed, together with accrued interest, at any time she wished. Rora Wood had a complicated mortgage history over the next 35 years but in 1866 Lewis Filmore acquired all the wood and coppice, estimated to be some 64 acres in extent. So by 1866 all the Rora estate was back under Lewis Filmore.

It is of interest to note that in the preceding year Lewis had agreed to pay a builder of Newton Abbot, Samuel Sercombe, £180 for altering a 'house at Rora' and this seems to have been a precursor of his intention to recover and improve the whole estate. Lewis married Theodosia Boyd, only daughter of Henry Clare, of Notting Hill, London and Worth in Sussex, in 1859. Upon his death in 1890 the estate passed to the surviving family,

Theodosia Boyd Filmore, her sons Lewis Egerton and Henry Clare, and her daughters Lucy Hill Carol Otway, Theodosia Catherine and Alice Boyd Bowers. Henry and Lucy died in 1910 and 1920 respectively and the estate passed to Lewis Egerton Filmore. In 1921 the estate was conveyed to Ralegh Buller Phillpotts of Bovey Tracey. Just after this conveyance Lewis made a declaration: 'My father the said Lewis Filmore was at the date of his death seised of both Rora Farm and Rora Wood free from encumbrances and that the same property has been in the possession of our family ever since and that no adverse claim has been made thereto by any person whomsoever.' (This was done because the documents relating to the ownership of Rora Farm had been lost.)

Ralegh Buller Phillpotts was descended from Henry Phillpotts, Bishop of Exeter, and was related through marriage to the Buller family whose most notable member was General Sir Redvers Buller V.C. Ralegh was called to the bar in 1894 and married Jean, youngest daughter of Alan Stewart of Kinloch, in 1898. He was created a knight in 1946 and died at Rora House in 1960. His widow moved with her son, Alan, to nearby Lenda and the farm was sold to Peter Aycliffe that same year and then a year later to Mr and Mrs McIlroy. At the time of writing Mrs McIlroy still resides there, her husband having died in 1998.

Rora House also passed from the Phillpotts family around 1960, firstly to Mr and Mrs Bradford and then to Malcolm Ford. From 1870 it became the headquarters of the Rora Christian Fellowship Trust.

The lands of Rora at the time of the tithe map of 1838 are as follows:

Field No.	Name	Type of Land	Size acres	roods	poles
434	Little or Lower Brake	A	4	2	12
435	Drews Marsh	A	3	2	2
436	Drews Marsh	W	0	2	12
437	Great or Square Brake	A	5	2	13
438	Jewell's Marsh	A	2	2	14
467	Gillwell	A	6	0	26
477	Rora Down	Down	44	1	32
478	Rora Down	Down	33	2	20
481	Woody Park	W	0	2	17
482	Woody Park	A	4	3	16
483	Middle Park	A	4	3	32
484	Colly Park	A	4	2	10
484a	Colly Park	C	0	1	8
485	Higher Meadow	P	3	0	6
485a	Higher Meadow	C	0	0	38
486	Rora House	House	0	1	32
487	Garden	G	0	0	31
488	New Plot	Plot	0	1	13
489	House and Road	House	0	2	36
490	Higher Orchard	O	0	3	5
491	Ley Piece	A	4	2	4

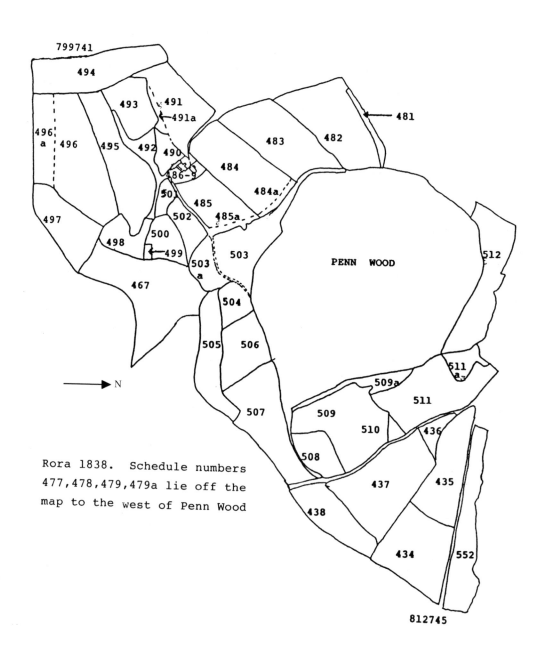

Fig. 5 *Map of the fields forming the Rora estate in 1838.*

491a	Ley Piece	W	0	1	4
492	Round Close	W	0	3	10
493	Round Close	A	2	0	8
494	Longland	A	4	4	6
495	Long Close	A	4	0	22
496	Buttons	C	5	3	22
496a	Buttons	A	1	3	0
497	Well Park	A	3	0	24
498	Well Park	C	1	1	26
499	Plot	C	0	0	17
500	Mead Plot	C	1	1	35
501	Lower Orchard	O	0	2	4
502	Lower Meadow	P	1	2	34
503	Nap Coppice & Waste	C	3	3	4
503a	Nap Coppice & Waste	Wood	1	0	16
504	Manna Park	O	1	0	8
505	Manna Park	A	2	1	16
506	Manna Park Moor	Rough Pasture	2	1	37
507	Manna Park Moor	Rough Pasture	4	2	31
508	White Ash	Alders etc.	1	1	22
509	White Ash	A	5	0	10
509a	White Ash	C	1	0	8
510	North Marsh	C	0	1	6
511	North Marsh	A	4	3	20
511a	North Marsh	C	0	3	29
512	Marley or Old Leys	Timber etc	4	1	24
552	Long Meadow	A	3	2	32
479	Rora Wood	C	44	3	2
479a	Rora Wood	Furze, Heath	18	0	36
		Total	254	0	32

A(Arable), C (Coppice), G (Garden), P (Pasture), W (Waste)

VI

The Church

A parish in early times was an area served by a church with a resident priest. The first known documentary mention of St Michael's Church, Ilsington is an undated charter, of about 1187, wherein John the Chanter, Bishop of Exeter, with the consent of his predecessor, Bishop Bartholomew, confirmed to the Prior and Convent of Plympton the 'Church of Elstinton'. That date, at the latest, may be taken as marking the formal start of Ilsington as an ecclesiastical parish but its boundary, as we have noted, was largely determined before that. No trace now remains of this first early church which probably consisted only of a small nave and chancel and might have been little more than a private chapel of the lord of the manor, probably a Beaumont. It is possible, but unproven, that there could have been a field church, that is a church without a graveyard, in pre-Conquest times.

On 6 June 1335 a licence was granted for the transference, by the Prior and Convent of Plympton, to John (Grandisson), Bishop of Exeter of the advowson of the 'churches of Ilstyngton, Stokyintynhide, Briddestowe, Bratton and Petrestavy in his diocese'. On 18 February, later changed to 2 October, 1338 a similar licence was granted to John for these advowsons to be transferred to the Wardens and Canons Secular of the newly founded college of 'Otery' and for the appropriations of the churches by the Warden and Canons. In that same year Bishop Grandisson assigned income from the tithes received to the college, save for £5 payable annually to Plympton. The Dean and Chapter of the college had no property of their own in Ilsington until 1490, when two of the Canons were granted lands in Staplehill by John ap Eynon. The College of St Mary was dissolved in 1545 and the living reverted to the Crown. In June 1545 the Earl of Hertford had foreknowledge that the lands of the college and several advowsons, including that of Ilsington, were to be offered to him on terms that were not sufficiently attractive and he declined the proposal. However, he did accept an offer which appears to be dated 20 May 1546 but there is no record that he ever paid any of the purchase money! In 1547, and now Duke of Somerset, he surrendered, *inter alia*, the advowson of Ilsington. On 7 October 1547 this was granted by Edward VI to the Dean and Canons of the Royal Free Chapel of St George, Windsor with whom the living still remains.

The Structure

No trace is apparent of the first church, built probably of cob and thatch. As time went by a structure more permanent and better suited to the slowly increasing prosperity of the parish was required. The earliest parts of this church still surviving, parts of the chancel and south transept, date from the late 13th and early 14th centuries but the south transept which is set at a marked angle to the rest of the church, may be early 13th-century. Further enlargement took place in the late 15th century while the church was under the auspices of the College of St Mary of Ottery. By then there was an increase in rural prosperity as villeins became yeomen holding their land as copyholders.

Major sources of local wealth lay in the woollen and cloth trades and in tin mining. In the more prosperous areas of the country, which included Devon, a strong natural church architecture arose, with Perpendicular-style windows, vaulting, fan tracery, wagon roofs and carved stalls. Ilsington was no exception and St Michael's Church took such a form, with a chancel with chapels to the north and south (the vestry chapel and lady chapel respectively), north and south aisles and transepts to the nave, and a tower some 70 feet high at the western end. Essentially this is the arrangement seen today, but there has been much restoration and maintenance over the years, sometimes carried out in a manner to be deprecated, which has inevitably led to changes and to some loss of features. These are now considered in turn.

In 1808 the roof was leaded, in 1822 the roof of the tower repaired and in 1823 the church, including the tower, roughcast. Repairs to the roof and ceiling were undertaken in 1830 and in the following year the plastering of the ceiling was completed. (Milles in 1750 reported that the church was not ceiled.) In 1856 it was resolved at a vestry meeting that C.H. Monro (Lord of the Manor of Ingsdon) should, *inter alia*, remove the layers of whitewash and white paint from the body of the church, the pillars and arches, and restore the screen. This 'whitening' had taken place in Puritan times no doubt to cover paintings of saints and the colouring of carvings. Unfortunately its removal destroyed these too. In 1856 a new ceiling was also put in the south aisle. In 1883 the church was closed for a major restoration following a very detailed specification drawn up by Mr E.C. Harbottle, architect, of County Chambers, Exeter. The major items were: the removal of the gallery and staircase at the west end of the nave; the removal of most of the pews and seating and wood flooring in the nave, aisles and transepts; the removal of granite flagging, doors, door frames and lath and plaster partition from the tower arch; the removal of the roughcast from exterior walls and buttresses of the south entrance porch and to repoint; to make provision for heating pipes; to remove all decayed stonework, including mullions and tracery to windows, and to make good with new; to construct a new belfry floor and to construct a partition between the vestry and organ chamber.

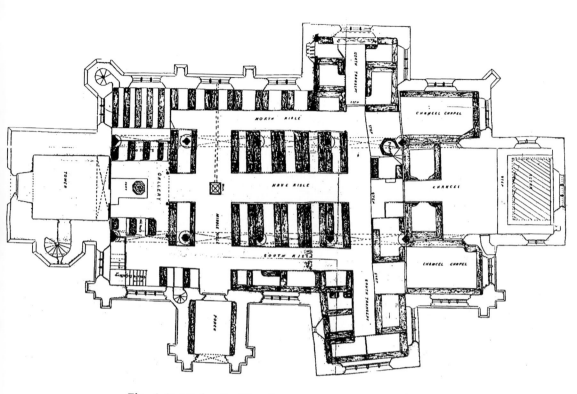

Fig. 6 *St Michael's Church prior to the 1883 restoration.*

It was stressed throughout that care must be taken to protect all stained glass, wood carving and other items which would be re-used, and no damage done to any carving, painting, colouring and fresco work. In 1909 a crucifix was designed by T.H. Lyon and placed on top of of the medieval screen over the chancel door. A figure of Jesus was added in 1921 in memory of Mr Woodley of Halshanger, and in 1962 the crucifix was removed from the screen and suspended from the roof. Further extensive repairs to roofs and woodwork were also carried out in 1954. In that year the chancel ceiling was repainted and the bosses decorated. In 1971 an aumbry was constructed in the wall of the lady chapel. Between the north and south aisles and the nave are five arcades, the pillars of which were hewn from single pieces of granite and are unusually slender. This, together with the width of aisles and nave, gives an air of spaciousness. Almost rounded granite arches rest on the pillars.

A main feature of architectural interest is the roofing seen in the interior of the church. Nave, chancel and north and south transepts all have wagon-roofs. In order to make the junction of longitudinal and transverse wagon-roofs possible the upper wall between the arcades and the nave roof in the fourth bay is left out and just a bridge remains. The vault of the central part of the roof of the nave springs from plain granite corbels. There are

12 images carved in oak in niches in these corbels, some with their faces gouged out. In 1875 Worthy believed that eight of these represented St Cecilia playing a musical instrument, St Dunstan with a harp, St James with the scallop, shell and pilgrim's staff, St Thomas with an arrow, St Helena with the Latin cross, St Lawrence with his grid-iron, St Jude with the club and St Michael, the patron saint of the church, with a trumpet.

On the centre line of the nave ceiling are two carved bosses which may represent King Henry VII and Queen Elizabeth of York. A third boss of three rabbits sharing three ears is a symbol adopted by tin miners and found also at Chagford and Widecombe. There are three others of bearded heads and one of a lion, representing King Henry VII, standing over a boar, depicting King Richard III defeated by Henry at Bosworth in 1485, and thus dating this part of the church to no earlier than that date. The boss is also surrounded by the roses of York and Lancaster, signifying the end of the Wars of the Roses and the union of these two houses by the marriage of Henry and Elizabeth. Pendant figures, which had been decapitated by the time of the visit by Worthy, had been restored to represent angels.

The tower was probably built when the church was enlarged in the 16th century. The 70 ft high tower is of three stages, unbuttressed, with a semi-octagonal stair turret half-way along the south side. Towers are clearly very exposed to the weather and the one at St Michael's is no exception. Over the years the stonework has been roughcast, repointed, roughcast again and repointed again in attempts to maintain a good appearance but also to help keep out the rain. The first known occasion for rendering was in 1823 and the last in 1955. In 1858 a new window was placed in the tower over the belfry door. In 1972 the rendering was removed and the masonry repointed and in 1996 repointed again on the west side and parts of the north and south sides: that is the condition today. In 1890 a new clock presented by Mrs Woodley in memory of her husband James Woodley of Halshanger was erected by John Smith of Derby. In 1914 the gallery under the tower was rebuilt as an organ chamber, in 1957 a new floor was laid in the bell-ringing chamber and in 1974 the interior of the stair turret was grouted to help keep it dry. Such an exposed feature as a tower will no doubt need much maintenance in the future. It has one three-light window of plain glass on the west.

A service of commemoration and thanksgiving was held on the 50th anniversary of V.E. day in 1995 and one on 3 November 2002 to mark all the recent work done, and funds raised, to maintain the fabric of the church.

The Windows

The earliest known documentary mention of windows dates only from 1750, when Milles states that in the east window of the south aisle is a 'beautiful coat-of-arms of Oldham and another which is now partly destroyed'. (Bishop Oldham was Bishop of Exeter from 1504-20.) Milles also refers to a window

showing the arms of Bishop Grandisson. The next known reference dates
from 1825 and is a brief desciption of a few pieces of stained glass with
heads of the Virgin in the chancel and, possibly, a depiction in the upper
window of the north aisle of the triumph of Christ over Islam.

In the early 1870s a more comprehensive description rather fortuitously
predated the major restoration of the church in 1883. At that time the north
chancel chapel (now the vestry chapel) had some remains of 15th-century
glass with heads of two saints, one of them representing the Magdalene, and
the upper portions of three elaborate canopies. The south chancel chapel
(now the lady chapel) contained the armorial bearings of the Munro (Monro)
family of Ingsdon on the three-light stained glass east window, as it does
today. The four-light south window fomerly had scenes from the Passion.
In the south transept there was an Early English lancet window in the west
wall depicting St George and also one showing the mutilated remains of an
old Perpendicular-style canopy. In the north window of the north transept
were the arms of Bishop Grandisson (1327-69), a shield divided into six
equal parts by stripes of silver and blue and a diagonal gold stripe, the whole
surmounted by a mitre between two eaglets with outstretched wings. Beneath
were the arms of the See of Exeter. The east window in the north transept
contained some remains of old stained glass in an advanced state of decay.
There were no descriptions of windows elsewhere in the church.

The vestry chapel was once the private chapel of Bagtor Manor and the
lady chapel that of the manor of Ingsdon. The lords of these two manors
would probably have borne the cost of their erection and they and their
families would have had exclusive seating rights within them. (In 1916
when the floor to the vestry chapel was relaid two stone memorials to the
Fords of Bagtor were found.) Before these two chancel chapels were built
there were Early English-style windows visible on two sides of the chancel.
Both windows have been partially blocked by these side chapels and small
square windows inserted and a priest's door added below.

Most of the old stained glass vanished during the restoration of 1883
but the arms of Bishop Grandisson were reset in the left-hand tracery of
the east window in the vestry chapel and those of the See of Exeter in the
right-hand tracery of that window. A new window depicting the Ascension
was placed in the north transept by George Wills of Narracombe in memory
of his wife Susanna (1815-60) and two sons John (1848-72) and Samuel
(1850-70). The chancel now has a three-light stained glass window in the
east wall depicting St Peter, the Virgin Mary and St Michael. The south
wall contains two plain glass two-light windows. The north wall has one
two-light window with plain glass. To the right of the altar is a piscina still
in use and in the floor commemorative ledger stones. The vestry chapel
now has, in the east wall, one three-light window of modern stained glass.
Built into the wall are fragments of stone with 'dog-tooth' mouldings. In
the north wall is a three-light window of plain glass. The south wall has a

four-light window of plain glass. In the three-light stained glass east window are the arms of the Munro family, and on the floor and walls memorials to the Beaumont and Pomeroy families. The east window of the north transept is now a three-light stained glass window set with a figure of St Michael dedicated by the Bishop of Crediton in memory of Lt Col Pitman of Green Lane, Ilsington churchwarden from 1947-56. The west wall of the transept has a single coloured light.

John Beaumont, who died in 1470, was the last of the Beaumonts of Ingsdon. His heir, as we have noted, was his daughter, Elizabeth, who married Robert Pomeroy and brought the estate to that family establishing some two centuries of Pomeroy ownership. Colesworthy was received by Elizabeth as a dowry on her marriage. At one time the south transept was a private chapel for this sub-manor of Colesworthy which was part of the Ingsdon estate. The estate was sold to the Woodleys of Halshanger who also had property in the Liverton area. In 1888 Mary Elizabeth, the daughter of John and Henrietta Divett, had built and filled with stained glass in the 'Crafts Revival style' a large four-light granite window in the south wall of the south transept; it is still there. She did this in memory of her parents who were a Bovey Tracey family that had once also owned Colesworthy. In 1960 the south transept was re-hallowed as a chapel dedicated to All Saints. The St Francis east window in this transept is now dedicated to the memory of Wilfred Potter of Haytor, one of the founders of the Tor bus service, a service proving of great benefit to the community for some thirty years.

The two windows in the south aisle are each of four lights of plain glass and the one in the west wall is of three lights and also plain. At the north-west corner of the north side is a five-sided stair turret with a single slit window. The windows in the north and south aisles are of Perpendicular style. The three in the north wall of the north aisle are each of three lights with modern coloured glass. The window in the west wall is of three-light plain glass. The two windows in the south wall of the south aisle are four-light plain glass and in the west wall three-light plain glass.

The Bells

In her *Notes on Devon Churches* Cresswell states, 'In 1553 theire were at Ilsyngton iiii belles yn the tower theire,' but unfortunately gives no reference as to where this statement originated. In 1750 Milles noted that there were four. Entries in the churchwardens accounts, which are only extant from 1779, show that they were in regular use from that date. There are entries recording the cost of new bell ropes in 1779 (5s.), 1784 (5s.) and 1786 (10s. 6d.). Bellringers were generally paid 5s. and the bells were rung routinely on the Coronation Day of King George III and on 5 November. One of the first entries has the ringers paid 2s. 6d. on the 'taking of the Spanish Fleet'. This would probably have been an action off Gibraltar which the French and Spanish fleets were blockading during the American War of Independence.

In 1795/6 four bells had to be taken down, re-cast and re-hung. This work was done by Bilbies of Cullompton at a cost of £95 2s. 6d. The newly cast bells were rung in 1797 to celebrate the victory over the Dutch fleet at Camperdown. Winslow Jones records that in 1825 there were five bells. In 1828 one bell weighing 610 lb was sold for 11d. a pound and replaced by another bought from William and Charles Pannel of Cullompton. This bell, of note C, weighed 690 lb and cost £43 2s. 6d. In 1870 the old treble bell, of note D, made by T. Bilbie of Cullompton in 1797, became cracked and a new one was bought from Messrs Meares and Stanbrook of London. In 1926 this treble bell also became cracked and was re-cast by Gillett and Johnston of Croydon, four others were a quarter re-tuned and an extra bell of note E was added to the peal of five. This, too, was made by Gillett and Johnston.

The bells were not rung from 1940-5. Then Gillett and Johnston inspected the oak beams from which the bells were hung, found them to be rotten and deemed it unsafe to ring the bells. In 1947 the bells were dismantled, appropriate repairs done, and then rehung on a new iron framework. They were re-dedicated by the former vicar, the Rev. Patch, and the current vicar the Rev. Collings. In 1963 a bell-chiming apparatus was installed which allowed two persons to ring the chimes. In 1998 the bearings of the bells were renewed and re-hung by Nicholson Engineering at a cost of £4,047.88. They were re-dedicated by the Bishop of Plymouth that same year. Details of the bells past and present, with their inscriptions, are shown below:

Bell 1. Note E. Diameter 27 inches, weight 493 lb. Gillett & Johnston, Croydon 1926. Ringers, C. Cox (Capt.) L. Clark, W. Redstone, A. Head, O. Roberts, F. Derges, W. Cox, E. Bourne, S. Roberts, J. Harvey, Vicar J.D.H. Patch.

Bell 2. Note D (the old treble). Diameter 29 inches, weight 566 lb. 'When I begin then all strike in; T. Bilbie, fecit 1797'. Recast 1870 Mears and Stanbrook, London. Wm Rowell & Thos Widger, wardens. Re-cast 1926 Gillett & Johnston, Croydon. R.W. Woodley & T.H. Lyon, wardens.

Bell 3. Note C. Diameter 33 inches, weight 653 lb. Wm & Chas Pannell Cullompton fecit. 1828. Charles C. Wills, John Rowell churchwardens.

Bell 4. Note B. Diameter 33 inches, weight 654 lb. Thos Bilbie Cullompton, fecit 1797. Rev. Jonathan Palk, vicar. Samuel Nosworthy & John Rowell, churchwardens.

Bell 5. Note A. Weight 802 lb. 'God Save the King'. T. B.F. 1797.

Bell 6. Note G. Diameter 42 inches, weight 1217 lb. Thomas Bilbie Cullompton fecit 1797. Rev. Jonathan Palk, vicar. Samuel Nosworthy & John Rowell, churchwardens.

The Reredos

The reredos was erected by Canon Percy Wise in memory of his wife, Caroline, formerly Caroline Lyon, who died suddenly on returning from Australia. It was designed by her brother T.H. Lyon of Middlecott and was shown in the exhibition of the Royal Academy and dedicated on the eve of Michaelmas in 1902. It was in three parts and contained fragments of old tracery found in a dealer's shop in Chagford which corresponded in character to parts of the screen. Originally it was behind the high altar in the chancel and covered up parts of the east window there. This position was not entirely popular and in November 2001 it was moved to be against the west wall of the south transept and allow major replastering in the chancel. Beneath it is the centre piece of the high altar bearing the inscription 'Behold the Lamb of God'. This was dedicated in 1964.

The Screen

The screen between the nave and chancel is probably 15th century in date but there is some doubt for parts seem to suggest the 16th century. It is of oak, richly carved, with a cornice and a triple frieze of foliage. Only traces remain of the colour which once adorned the figures of saints upon it.

The Pulpit

The present pulpit is modern but traditional in style, the carvings reflecting those of the rood screen. It replaced an earlier one removed at the 1883 restoration. The latter had a canopy, or sounding-board, taken down by the curate in the 1850s. There was some controversy over this but a poll of parishioners in 1857 agreed that it should not be replaced.

The Vicar's Stall

Just behind the pulpit is a fine stall made up in 1883 from medieval bench-ends and pews known as 'poppy-heads'. This design is rare in Devon although another is thought to have been, at least in 1825, in St Mary's, Atherington. The east side of the stall bears the coat-of-arms of the Beaumont/Pomeroys, the alliance of which families has already been noted.

The Lectern

This, too, is modern but in traditional style and was presented to the church in 1934 in memory of Brennan Dyball, surgeon, who lived at 'Boulders', a bungalow at Haytor, and who was buried at Ilsington in that year.

The Font

This octagonal granite font has a plain plinth, shaft and bowl and is thought to be medieval in date and the oldest fitment in the church. In 1812 stone from Haytor was used for the flooring by the font.

The Music Gallery

Today the music gallery houses the organ but the churchwardens' accounts show that in early times musical accompaniment was provided by viols, a group of stringed instruments. There were numerous entries for expenses incurred in their repair and for the instruction of singers:

> 1779 Mending the Base Viol and carriage £1. 2s. 0d.
> 1794 Richd Taylor for instructing the Singers 10s. 6d.
> 1797 Strings for the Viols and Gluing the Trible [*sic*] Viol £1.

There seem to have been four viols. In 1822 these were augmented by a flute:

> Josias Rowell for a new flute £1. 3s.

Robert Lovett became the vicar in 1867 and soon after acquired an organ which was placed in the gallery at the west end of the nave. Before the 1883 restoration it extended in width to the pillars of the nave and out into the church nearly to the crossing of the aisles. It was some eight feet above the ground and reached by a flight of stairs from the lady chapel. The small organ was placed in the centre. An early reference to the gallery is in 1805, when William Ball had a contract to break down the old gallery and build a new one, and in 1810 new pews were erected in front of the gallery. The specification for the major restoration in 1882 called for the removal of the

7 Medieval font, St Michael's church

8 *St Michael's Church, south porch and tower.*

gallery and staircase at the west end of the nave except for the organ and fittings. Two years later the north chancel chapel (priest's vestry), then the family pew for Bagtor, was handed back for an organ chamber and a new organ installed by Mr Hawkins of Newton Abbot. It was used for that purpose until 1914 when the present organ-loft was built in the gallery under the tower, notwithstanding a proposal the year before to move it to the north transept. Parishioners voted by 139 to 60 to reject that proposal but agreed not to oppose the organ's going elsewhere. In 1901 it was re-dedicated, and in 1954 it was overhauled and the gallery extended.

The South Porch

This was built in early Tudor times of granite and local stone rubble probably obtained from a quarry at Middlecott. It is battlemented and buttressed and two storeys in height. A priest's room over the porch is reached from inside the church and was used, it is said, by the priest from St Mary Ottery who came over for the Sunday Mass and spent the night there. It may also have been used as a parish strong room for valuables and church records. Over the door outside are three niches. The centre one housed a figure of Our Lady. (The present figure of Virgin and Child is 20th century and brought from Bruges and has the emblem of lily and thorn at each side.) Above are the Old English characters MXT, the fleur de lys and R. It is thought that these are the initial letters of Petitions from the Litany of Loretto, namely:

Mater Christi – Mother of Christ
Terris Eburnea – Tower of Ivory
Flos Florum – Flower of Flowers
Regina Coeli – Queen of Heaven

The left-hand niche has S and A on either side for St Anne, mother of the Virgin. The letters on the right-hand side have disappeared. Stone benches in the porch are where secular and ecclesiastical business of the parish was conducted.

The West Lychgate

Over the west gate of the churchyard there was an ancient room about ten feet from the ground which for a short while before 1639 served as a schoolroom but in that year collapsed (see Chapter IX). Clearly it must have been rebuilt for in 1871 the vestry minutes show that it was decided to pull down the room, then known as the vestry room, over the lychgate because of its dilapidated condition. The modern lychgate and room above were designed by Mr T.H. Lyon of Middlecott and built in 1910. The statue of St George is part of a First World War monument and underneath is the 'Brasparts' plaque presented by the people of that town in Brittany with which Ilsington was twinned.

The Incumbents

c.1255 – c.1280	William
c.1297	Roger de Otery
– c.1310	Peter de Cornu
c.1310 – 1318	Peter de Honetone
1318 –	John de Lustleigh
– 1342	Richard de Langacre
1342 – 1349	William de Doderidge
1349 – 1349	Alexander Perkyn
1349 – 1375	Thomas Burgeys
1375 – 1391	Robert Langebrook
1391 –	Thomas Wythyman
– 1438	William Cracow
1438 – 1439	William Bousquyer
1439 – 1444	William Cracow
1444 – 1479	John More
1479 – 1494	John Drake
1494 – 1500	Robert Festham
1500 –	Thomas Furneaux
– 1532	Hugh Bruseigh
1532 – 1544	Oliver Smyth
1544 – 1562	Robert Tuckfield
1562 – 1562	David Trevor
1562 – 1577	William Byckford
1577 – 1585	George Swete
1585 – 1597	Benedict Parker
1597 – 1597	John Lambert
1597 – 1621	Radford Maverick
1621 – 1626	Christopher Warren
1626 – 1634	Thomas Clifford
1634 – 1645	Robert Dove
1646 – 1653	Humphry Dyer
1653 – 1662	Robert Stooke
1663 – 1664	William Bettenson
1664 – 1668	Richard Bryan
1688 – 1710	William Risdon
1711 – 1715	Armand Dubourdier
1715 – 1739	Philip Nanson
1739 – 1745	John Petvin
1745 – 1748	Thomas Rayne
1748 – 1749	Jeremy Pemberton
1749 – 1786	Charles Bedford
1787 – 1789	George Stevenson
1790 – 1825	Jonathan Palk
1826 – 1867	Charles Marsham
1867 – 1875	Robert Lovett
1875 – 1879	Thomas Braim
1879 – 1898	Thomas Hale
1898 – 1908	William Fox
1908 – 1932	John Patch
1932 – 1939	George Newton
1939 – 1952	Herbert Collings
1952 – 1958	Bernard Smith
1959 – 1972	John Donaldson
1972 – 1986	Derrick Reynolds
1987 – 1993	Michael Glare
1993 – 2004	Clifford Curd

The Churchwardens

No comprehensive list of churchwardens is extant and if it were would run into many hundreds of names for at least two are appointed every year. Some 17th-century holders, their dates as shown in the parish registers, follow:

1603 Thomas Nosworthye
1605 Hugh Pynsent
1608 John Bowden
1634 Rob Oland, Jo Courtier, Richard Andrewes, Edward Forde, Thomas Northway, William Degon, John Bickley, John Gosswill
1636 William Wotton
1637 Robert Smerdon

1638 William Smerdon, Richard Weeger
1639 John Lambshead, Richard Stancombe
1640 John Wotton
1653 Hannibal Corbyn (Register), Thomas Reynell
1679 John Cortier (Register)
1683 Edward Tucker (Register)

The Memorials

The most intriguing memorial is a mutilated limestone effigy of a recumbent woman in the north transept. There have been many theories as to whom she may represent. The north transept is generally accepted as being of the late 13th or early 14th century and it would be reasonable to suppose that the figure post-dates that period. It could be a wife or close relative of a Dynham, which family held Ilsington from at least 1284 to 1501. There is much to be said, however, for it being the effigy of Isabella de Fishacre. She was the grandmother of John Dynham (born 1295, died 1332). Moreover, in 1303 she herself held Ilsington jointly with John de Beaumond and the Lay Subsidy rolls for 1332 show an Isabella de Fishacre as the most wealthy person in the parish. Of course, the Isabellas of 1303 and 1332 may not be the same person but it is reasonable to suppose that they were. If so, her long association with Ilsington, together with a death likely to have been in the early 14th century, makes her a strong candidate.

There are well over six hundred memorials within or outside the church which are still readable. The earliest of these is to Hugh Bruseigh. A free translation of the Latin inscription reads: 'Under this stone lies Master Hugh Bruseigh, formerly vicar of this church and of the church at Widecombe who died on the 27th day of October in the year of the Lord 1532'. An interesting 17th-century memorial to Thomas Ford of Sigford, Ilsington is in the form of a chromogram: 'Deposit um Thomae Ford de Sigford gen qui obijt decimo nono die Noviembris Chromogramma DorMIo et Vrspero CIneres sIne Labe res Vrgent'. The capital letters DMIVCIILV when rearranged give the date of death: MDC (1600) LVVIII (63).

The memorial to Thomas Pomeroy, Lord of the Manor of Ingsdon, is phrased in somewhat ornate terms, a free translation from the Latin being:

> 1610 Here lies the body of Thomas Pomeroy of Ingsdon Knight who died the 18th of April in the year of our salvation one thousand six hundred and ten which was the sixty first of his life. Behold King of Kings you gave the royal fruit Pomeroy and you pluck it for he who bears the fruit let him reap it. Life is the way to death and death is the gateway to life. That death which took my life to me was life.

The last date of an inscription in Latin is on the tomb of Robert Dove and his son Matthew and daughter Frances from 1645.

As might be expected there are memorials to the families who owned the manors comprising the parish of Ilsington, namely the Pomeroys, Battishills, Hale Munros and Tothills, and to the benefactors of the parish charities. In the lady chapel there are memorials to Seymour Vassal Hale Munro, Louisa Maxwell, Charles Hale Munro and his wife Mary Jane, and Seymour Charles Hale Munro and in the churchyard is a cross to Charles James Hale Munro.

There are 11 tombs and headstones which are 'listed monuments'. With the dates of death and/or burial these are:

Thomas Ford (chromogram)
Edward Ford 1665
Sibyll Southcote and also Mary 1674
Edward Ford of Sigford 1674
Grace Furlong 1686
George Hart and Agnes Hart 1642 and Amy Northway 1644
Mary Codner 1672
Mary Bound 1677
Eliza Weeger 1759
Elizabeth Laskey 1702
Ambrose and George Campion

Taxation

In 1253 Pope Innocent XXII gave first fruits and tenths to Henry III for three years, which gave rise to a taxation known as the Valor of Pope Innocent. In 1288 Pope Nicholas IV granted the tenths to Edward I for six years to help towards defraying the expenses for an expedition to the Holy Land. A taxation was begun in that year by the King's Precept and finished, as to the province of Canterbury, in 1291. The liability to this tax for Ilsington and some neighbouring churches was:

Ilsington £14 12s. 4d.
Widecombe £14 4s. 0d.
Manaton £4 13s. 4d.

In the 26th year of King Henry VIII's reign (1535) a Valor Ecclesiasticus sought to obtain knowledge of the yearly value, both spiritual and temporal, of all religious bodies in England and Wales and superseded that of Nicholas IV. Returns were made to a body which bore the splendid name of the Court of First Fruits and Tenths. Both the vicarial and rectorial parts of Ilsington were covered. The vicarage (Oliver Smyth, vicar) was shown as worth £17 9s. 5½d. with tithes of 34s. 11½d. The detailed returns included such items as wool, sheep, hay and pension payments by the Master of the College of the Blessed Mary of Ottery and his successors. (The detailed returns in fact totalled £19 9s. 6½d.) The rectory was stated to be worth £15 2s. which included, *inter alia*, payments for the souls of Sibilla, mother of Bishop Grandisson, formerly Bishop of Exeter, Katherine his sister and William his father.

VII

TERRIERS AND TITHES

In 1636 the vicar of Ilsington, Robert Dove, compiled a terrier, an inventory or register of land belonging to the vicarage. The terrier was recorded in the parish registers and reads:

> A Terriour of the gleabe land belonging to the Vicarage of Ilstingtonne
> The Church litten containing a quarter of an acre
> The houses garden and Orchard – one acre
> The Swyne pyke – thirty acres or thereabout
> The Down pyke – eighteene acres or thereabout
> The Broom pyke – five acres
> The Middle pyke – five acres
> The Higher Marell pyke – two acres and a halfe
> The Middle Marell pyke – two acres
> The Meadowe – one acre
> The North pyke – three acres
> The Long Marell pyke – one acre and a halfe
> The Poole pyke – one acre
> Robt Dove vicar
> Ch wardens John Bowden William Wotton This Glebe Land was viewed and estimated by they whose names are under wrighted Aprill 19

In 1727 the vicar Philip Nanson was also required by the Bishop of Exeter to complete a terrier. He returned the following information:

> The Vicarage House is built partly with slate stones and partly with moor stones and covered partly with shingles. It consists of twelve upper rooms, including closets, all floored with boards and ceiled. And three of the said rooms are about half wainscoted. It consists also of twelve lower rooms all ceiled or lathed and plastered except one which is under the Parsonage House. One of the said rooms, viz.the Parlour, is floored with boards and about half wainscoted. There is a barn thereunto belonging of 40ft. in length, a stable and sheep-pen united of about 41ft. in length, and a linney adjoining them on the east side 32ft. in length, and a Necessary House at the north end of the Mansion House. They are all built with moor and slate stones and covered with reed.

Nanson then repeated the terrier of Robert Dove, following which he continued:

Swine park is divided into four fields, two arable and two furze ground, and adjoins to Coxland tenement on the south side, to Widdicombes tenement on the west side and to the highway on the north and east sides. Downpark is divided into five fields, all arable ground, and adjoins to Hunnevil tenement on the south and to the highway on the other sides. Broompark, Middle park, Hr. and Md. Marell Parks and the Meadow are all contiguous and are bounded by the vicarage barn and Cowses tenement on the east, and by highways on the west end and both sides. Lr. Marell Park, arable ground, is bounded on the north by the highway and otherwise by Mr. Charles Corbyn's land.

North Park and Long Marell Park, the former furze and the latter arable, adjoin each other and are bounded by the highway on the E and S sides and by Mr. John Drake's land on the W and N.

Pool Park, arable ground, is bounded by Narracombe on the north, by Court Barton on the east and by Centory Ground on the south and west sides.

The Glebe has a right of common appertaining to it for all sorts of cattle, and it is not limited to any certain number of cattle of any sort.

The fences of the Church Litten are stone walls, repaired when there is occasion by a Parish Rate. There is one timber tree on the glebe, an oak in the Meadow, worth about 15s. and ten elms in the Church Litten worth about 15s. apiece, and no others.

The surplice fees are as follows, 2d. a head annually for every person of 16 years and over for the Easter Offering; marrying 2s. 6d.; churching 6d.; burying 1s. There is belonging to the church a silver salver of 8oz. weight with the inswcription on it 'Ex dono P.N.V.Ilsington A.D.1720', and a silver chalice and coverlid of 13¾oz. together, with the word 'Pons' at the bottom of both of them. Also a pewter flagon, bason and plate, a pall, a bier and four bells.

The church and churchyard are repaired at the expense of the parishioners, the chancel at the expence of the Rector. The clerk and sexton are appointed by the Vicar, but are both paid by the parish. The former's salary is 40s. a year, and the latter's is 10s. for looking after the bells, 5s. 6d. for sweeping the church, 1s. 6d. a year for cleaning the churchyard and 5s. for whipping dogs out of the church at the time of Divine Service.

The terrier was signed by the churchwardens, Richard Lear and Nathaniel Bickford, and the vicar on 27 March and witnessed by R. Tapson, Richard Widdecombe sen., Thos. Rowell, Michael Cummin, Edward Taylor and John Bowdon.

In 1920 the glebe lands were sold at auction by Messrs Rendell and Sawdye. At that time the fields, their names and their sizes (converted to acres from acres, roods and poles) were as follows:

Lot 1. Long Park 1.47 acres.
Lot 2. Bush Park, Middle Park and Broom Park plus cottage gardens etc. totalling 18.42 acres.

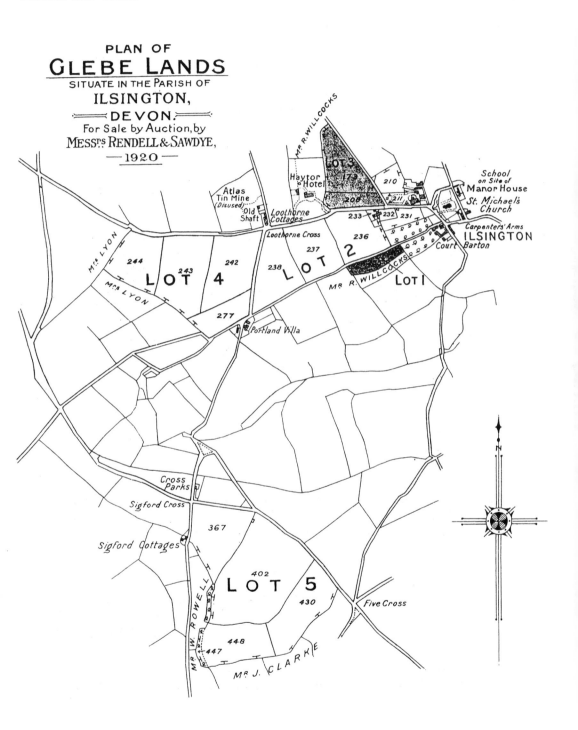

Fig. 7 *Plan of the Glebe lands.*

Lot 3. Marl Park and North Park totalling 7.37 acres.
Lot 4. Great, Middle, Higher and Lower Down Parks totalling 26.0 acres.
Lot 5. Swine Park plus a copse 39 acres.

It will be seen that the total area of these lands is considerably more than that given by Robert Dove. This is likely to be due to the relative inaccuracy of the early measurements rather than an augmentation in real terms.

In early times one tenth of the increase in all living crops and livestock was paid to the church. The village priest did not fare well in this system for a practice which became standard was the impropriation, that is incorporation, of a church into a monastery or later into a cathedral or diocese. The impropriator kept the bulk of the tithes, the great tithes, but was obliged to provide for a priest to undertake the local ecclesiastical duties. That priest took the small tithes and a portion of the glebe which could be let or used. He was then known as a vicar. A rector was a parish incumbent who received all the tithes, both great and small. In general the rectorial tithes went to the cathedral or diocese to help keep the latter in sound financial shape. The impropriator, however, was expected to use the rectorial tithes for appropriate charitable purposes and as a general church fund.

It is fair to conjecture that the Reverend Nanson, vicar from 1715 to 1739, was unusual in his determination to receive all his dues. The following two entries taken from the Ilsington parish registers show that he was a vicar with a developed financial understanding. This entry was made in the registers by Nanson on 20 February 1722:

Thomas Tothill of Bagtor paid me by virtue of a composition under his hand the sum of £5 10s. 0d. per annum for the small tithes of his barton of Bagtor from Michaelmas 1716 to 1719 and in that composition he compounded expressly with me for the tithe of the toll of Bagtor Mills as for his other small tithes. The year following, his tenant Anthony Edwards would not pay me for Bagtor Mills, whereupon I exhibited a libel against him in the Consistory Court at Exon for the tithe of the toll of all sorts of corn ground and of clover seed shelled at the said mills. He then yielded to pay me without proceeding to an Answer, both my charges in giving him there and for the tithe of the toll. The sum he paid me in lieu of the tithe of the toll was 28 shillings, which was after the rate of 2s. in the £ according to the rent he paid Thomas Tothill. After that he paid me the tithe of his mills in kind, which was what he called the tenth toll of wheat, malt, barley and oats (which my servant Henry John fetched thence) or otherwise the tenth penny if he was paid in money for grinding any corn. Afterwards Sarah Zellack rented those mills for some time and being I found I could get but little by taking the tithe of those mills in kind, I compounded with her for 20s. per annum in lieu. This I record here for the Remembrance of my successors in order to preserve their right for ever, and that they were disputed when the tithes of Ingsdon Mills, of Liverton Mills and of Pool Mill was all along paid me peaceably.

In March 1727 another entry continues the saga of his tithes:

> The Vicarage consists of the tithes of grass, hay and all grass seeds, both the first as well as the second shear when they are cut twice down the same year. Likewise of colts, calves, lambs and pigs in kind, if there shall ten of either sort fall in one year and live to be weanable, otherwise of the tenth part of the value of what number under that shall happen to fall that year. Otherwise the Incumbent at election may wait another year for his tenth. It consists also of the tithe of wool, honey, carrots, turnips, and potatoes and of apples, pears and fruit trees sold or transplanted. Also of the tithes of profits of agistments and of all sorts of corn ground at Bagtor, Ingsdon, Levaton and Pool Mills which are all the watermills that lie within the parish of Ilsington.
>
> Mr Thomas Tothill of Bagtor, Richard Widdicombe sen. and jun. of Horridge, John Wills of Smallacombe, John Bowdon of Brimley and divers other inhabitants bound themselves under a penal obligation about the year 1717 to pay the small tithes of their estates in kind to me. Other tithes of the Vicarage consist of one penny to be paid yearly by each house-holder to the Vicar, commonly called a Garden Penny, and another penny to be paid yearly by each house-holder called a Hearth Penny.
>
> There is a Pretended Prescription to pay two milk in the year to the Vicar, viz. the milk of all kine the week before Midsummer and the week before Michaelmas in lieu of the tithe of milk for the whole year, but I never complied with it in any place throughout the said parish. I never had the tithe of any coppice wood in kind nor ever found that the Vicarage was endowed with it, but I searched the Bishop's Registry and was advised that the custom of a Hearth Penny at Ilsington would be a bar to my recovery to the tithe of coppice wood.

As time went by there was a general discontent over the payment of tithes – and a fear by tithe owners that the increasing enclosure of land might lead to loss of income from problems in apportionment of responsibility as well as the impracticability of payment by product. A national attempt to commute tithes to a single rent charge was adopted in 1836 and tithe commissioners were appointed to administer it. An agreement for such a commutation in Ilsington parish was reached on 7 June 1838 following a survey. Peter Gillard, land surveyor of Stokenham, apportioned the rent charge as follows:

> Gross rent charge payable to the tithe owner in lieu of tithes ... including tithe of glebe £640 10s. (a further total rent charge of £7 10s. 0d. was also payable when the glebe lands were not in the occupation of the rectors and vicars.)
> To the vicar £302 12s. 8d.
> To the appropriate rectors and their lessee £344 17s. 4d.
> Value in imperial bushels, and decimal parts of an imperial bushel, of wheat, barley and oats.
> Wheat 7s. 0¼d. a bushel (614.83679 bushels)

Barley 3s. 11½d. a bushel (1090.52631 bushels)
Oats 2s. 9d. a bushel (1569.69697 bushels)

The total acreage of the parish was given as 7,563 acres and 10 perches, which included arable, meadow, orchard, common and furze, coppice and woodland, waste, timber and buildings. Not all was subject to the payment of tithes; for example, coppice and woodland and the glebe lands of the appropriate rectory and of the vicarage. The area of land subject to tithes was given as follows:

Arable land 2,714 acres
Meadow or pasture land 654 acres
Orchard land 130 acres
Common and furze land 1,662 acres

The appropriate rectors for Ilsington were the Canons of Windsor. The glebe lands of the vicarage still bore the names of Great, Lower, Home and Higher Swine park; Higher, Middle, Little, Great and Lower Down park; Broom park; Middle park; Bush park; North park; Pule park; Long park and Marl park, containing by estimation 77 acres. The names and the total area are close to those recorded in the 1636 terrier but with some sub-division of the fields. There were other small pieces of land extending to about three acres. The glebe lands of the rectory were three pieces of arable land called the Sentry Ground, containing ten acres and two roods, a parcel of meadow in front of the parsonage house of one acre and one rood and another of one rood.

The Tithe Redemption Commission administered new Acts of 1936 and 1951 to commute rent charges to a lump sum which could be paid in instalments.

VIII

CHARITIES

The Bequest of Jane Ford

It was a common practice from early times for parishioners to leave money in their wills for the benefit of the poor. Land and buildings might also be left either for sale or for rent, the proceeds again to be used for charitable purposes. Such property was placed in the hands of trustees, or feoffees as they were sometimes known, with suitable arrangements made for further trustees to be appointed when this became necessary.

Jane Ford was born at Bagtor House around 1584, the youngest daughter of Thomas Ford and Elizabeth Popham and sister to John Ford, the Elizabethan dramatist. In her will of 24 November 1663 she devised to William Culling, Thomas Ashford and Henry Nosworthy and their heirs two enclosed fields within the parish of Ashburton upon trust. The rents and profits derived from these would be used to keep poor children in the parish of Ilsington at school and to pay for their teaching until they could read the Bible. The children were to be chosen by the trustees with the advice and consent of the churchwardens and the overseers of the parish. Jane left the trustees an annuity of £6 for use until they were able to take possession of the two fields. The fields were of about four acres and two acres in extent.

Trustees died and were replaced over the years, often by those related to the Ford family. By 1793 a trust deed showed that Thomas Brown occupied the four-acre field at a rent of £12 a year and William Kingwell the other at £9 a year. In 1798 and 1799 prayer books, spelling books and bibles were bought for a cost of £4 10s. 7d. and in 1820 100 bibles were bought for £25 3s. 0d. By 1865 gross income had been reduced to £18 10s. 0d. and this was used to buy books and to pay teachers. By 1900 a new scheme drawn up by the Charity Commissioners required that children must be *bona fide* residents of Ilsington, have been scholars for two years, be of good conduct and be regular attenders. The trustees were to ensure that their general progress had been satisfactory. By 1964 the two fields, Lenghill and Cross Parks, were still held on trust and providing an income of around £30 p.a. Today only Cross Parks is still producing a rent for charitable purposes and this goes towards the purchase of books and equipment for the two Ilsington schools.

The Parish Lands

Another early charity, and perhaps the earliest in Ilsington, was known as that of the Parish Lands and consisted of property to be used for 'the better Maintenance and Reliefe of such of the said poore as shall be visited with sickness such as shall be aged and stricken in years and such as shall be impotent as thereby utterly disabled to worke'. These properties consisted of a building called the Church or Parish House and an adjoining plot of land some 86 feet by 24 feet in size and a garden. This house was adjacent to St Michael's Church. Such church houses generally evolved from the brew-houses of the lords of the manor and the earliest can be dated at least from the 12th century. The poor house at Ilsington probably evolved around the start of the 16th century. The earliest known document relating to the endowment of these properties is dated 22 March 1695 and names the surviving trustees as Peter Woodley of Ashburton, Humphry Degon, Francis Furlong, William Smerdon, James Arthur, John Rowell, Edward Furlong, Henry Lambshead, Richard Stancomb, Richard Weaver and John Leate. However, the church house was mentioned in the survey of Dynham lands in 1566.

On 23 January 1823 a report on the status of charities in Ilsington showed the properties to consist of a dwelling house, outhouses, garden and orchard adjoining the highway from Bickington to Bovey Tracey, with a lease granted to Stephen Laskey, a house and garden leased to William Osmond, and a house and garden leased to James Chalker. All were situated at Hartford in Ilsington parish. A further two houses and a garden at Cold East near Ilsington Heathfield were leased to John Northway and later assigned to George Laskey. There were also two fields in the occupation of James Southward. In addition to these was the church house itself, used as a poor house with a small court adjoining.

When trustees were appointed in 1803 they found the affairs of the trust in much disorder, with buildings in need of repair, some buildings and fields occupied illegally and with no payments of rent. Although legal steps were taken to rectify these failures in administration they met with limited success, for by 1823 some of the new lessees still refused to pay on the grounds that the enclosure of Ilsington Heathfield in 1809 had destroyed their time-honoured rights to cut furze and heath. Moreover, some of the fees raised upon granting of the new leases had been placed in the bank of a Mr Abraham of Ashburton which failed in 1812. The expenses incurred by the trustees in putting affairs on a better footing meant that there could be no distribution of funds to the poor until 1807. One must feel sympathy with the necessary, but unpopular, actions of the trustees, worthy souls who were putting right the inefficiencies of others.

When all was in better order income payments were resumed to those poor persons selected, following what was known as 'examination for settlement'. In the late 18th and early 19th centuries it was important to determine to

9 *Rear of St Michael's Cottages.*

which parish a person belonged for the parish had to maintain those without adequate means of sustenance. There are in existence for Ilsington parish some two hundred records of such examinations. Two typical examples are shown below:

1780 Clement Leamen labourer of Ilsington born in Widecombe. At 14 went to live as non-indentured apprentice to Thomas Winsor of Staverton until 20 years old. Returned to Widecombe as labourer for several years, married there but now resides in Ilsington as labourer.

1812 Elizabeth Terry widow of Ashburton born in Highweek, parents' legal settlement being Ilsington. Married John Terry who worked at the claypits in Kingsteignton. Has never lived as servant, never knew where husband was born or belonged or came from. Has not heard from husband for three years but saw him board H.M.Frigate at Portsmouth about five years ago. Been informed since he was lost in H.M.Ship *Crescent*.

The poor house was where numbers 1 and 2 St Michael's Cottages now stand and the brew-house was at number 3. The earliest record of expenditure on the poor house is in 1813, when two loads of wood were bought for 5s. 6d.

In 1815 a vestry meeting decided to make the following allowances for the poor. Sundays: for breakfast seven ounces of bread with broth for the men and five ounces of bread and butter with one teaspoon full of tea for the women. Dinner was seven ounces of bread with broth, half a pound of pudding, four ounces of a leg of mutton with roots and vegetables. Supper was five ounces of bread, three ounces of cheese with half a pint of cider, or seven ounces of bread with broth and tea as for breakfast for the women and children. On Mondays there was bread and broth for both breakfast and supper and for dinner seven ounces of bread with broth and half a pound of pudding and four ounces of beef with roots and vegetables. On Tuesdays once again the ubiquitous bread and broth was served for breakfast; dinner consisted of one pound of suet pudding with vegetables and half a pint of cider, and supper was five ounces of bread and three ounces of cheese with yet another half a pint of cider. The diet for the rest of the week was entered in the records as 'Thursdays and Satterdays. The Meat alike. Mondays, Wednesdays and Fridays, Do. And those that work to have ten ounces of Bread and six ounces of Cheese and one pint of Cyder'. It all seems stodgy but filling and not ungenerous for the 'social security' of two centuries ago.

At a vestry meeting on 24 March 1828 it was decided to borrow £200 on the security of the parish to do essential repairs and maintenance on the poor house and also to build cottages for use as occasional poor houses for those termed the 'out-poor'. The maintenance included a room to be set aside for the resting of coffins and another to be converted into a strong room for the secure confinement of inmates. Another alteration was to incorporate the adjoining brew-house into the poor house. The new cottages for the out-poor were built at Smokey Cross and still exist, having undergone some changes with the years. The first known occupants were Joseph Cock, Eliza Cotman, Ann Spry and Sarah Vallance.

In 1834 the Poor Law Amendment Act transferred the administration of the Poor Law from some 15,000 parishes to 643 specially created unions each with a workhouse. Ilsington parish then came under Newton Abbot. The occupants of the cottages at Smokey Cross moved in 1836 and an entry in the poor book shows 'Mr Charles Wills for 2 horses and carts for taking the poor to Newton to be examined 10s.' and, later, 'Paid the Overseer of Ashburton for taking the poor to Newton belonging to Ilsington ... Paid for the refreshments for the poor when at Newton £1. 7s. 0d.'

The numbers of those in the poor house at Ilsington varied from nine to 18 but many more, never fewer than fifty, were given monthly relief. After the removal of the parish poor it was agreed in 1839 that the poor houses near the church should be converted into three cottages and then sold and those at Smokey Cross also sold. A century later those by the church were condemned as unfit for human habitation. They were saved from demolition by a Captain Quelch who bought them with the sole intention of putting them into a fit state for sale, which he duly achieved. The property of the Parish Lands now consists of Candy Cottage, the Great Twinnabrooks fields near the Liverton playing fields, Grammar Close and Parish Meadow. These bring in an annual rental which, together with the capital sums raised by the sales, is invested for the purposes of the charity.

The Candy Trust

On 17 November 1727 William Candy of Hartford, Ilsington made a will which included clauses to benefit some of the poor in the parish. Candy is believed to have been a travelling fiddler who settled in Hartford and became a farmer. After the usual provisions for debts, funeral expenses and modest legacies he bequeathed his estate at Hartford, also known as Hore's Tenement, to the vicar and churchwardens with Robert Tapson, Richard Lear and Richard Widdicombe junior as trustees. He made provision for the appointment of new trustees as became necessary (and bequeathed £10 for the trustees to buy mourning rings!). His will went on to declare:

> I bequeath every year on the 21st December called St Thomas Day to nine poor men of Ilsington of sober life and conversation, who resort to the Parish Church on the Lord's Day, a new Hat, a new Cloth Coat, a new Shirt, a new pair of Shoes. The poor men are to be chosen by my Trustees.
> I also give 9 shillings every year to be expended on Meat and Drink between the nine poor men on Christmas day at the Church House after prayers and sermon are ended.

The money for these charitable gifts was to come from the income received from lands purchased by the trustees with the sum of £200 left by William Candy (less 20 shillings annually to be paid to the vicar for preaching a sermon on the anniversary of his death). It took nearly forty years before suitable property could be purchased and until then any income was derived from investment in a mortgage. Two properties called Gillhill and Killa were purchased for £220 and it seems that the churchwardens at that time, Charles Corbyn and Joseph Wills, paid the extra £20 from their own funds. The report of the Charity Commissioners in 1823 stated that the two properties were of a combined size of some 23 acres and 18 poles.

By that date the trustees had found it appropriate not to limit the benefits to nine men but to purchase shoes, shirts, hats and coats for as many men not in receipt of constant relief as the total charitable income could provide. As many as 32 were assisted in 1820 and in 1821. The nine shillings bequeathed for meat and drink was also used for clothing. By 1865 the total income received from all the Candy properties was £61 8s. 6d. of which £1 went to the vicar for preaching the service. By an order of the Charity Commissioners dated 15 January 1897 the charity was divided into two parts to be known as the church part and the poor part. The former comprised the £1 to the vicar who referred to the gift in his Christmas service. In August 1900 part of the Candy lands was conveyed to the trustees of Blackpool School but the rest remained the same as in 1823 and was let to Mr Hellier for £47 a year.

There were, of course, expenses involved in fulfilling the terms of the charity, including the purchase of a cloth known as 'kersey' or 'parson's gray' for the coats and 'dowlas' for the shirts, and also for travelling expenses of the tailors involved. The benificent William Candy, too, had to be properly laid to rest and the first expense was to pay 'Jonathan Luscombe for Mr Candy's coffin £1 7s. 6d.' and, on a lighter note, for 'an Hogshead of Cider for his funeral'.

Two world wars and the advent of a national social security system made changes in the detail of the awards inevitable, and the provision of boots, hats and shirts ceased. Coats were still provided and also gifts of food, assistance with fuel bills and, indeed, general help to parishioners in need at any time. As time passes these, too, will probably be superseded by other means of assistance.

Bequest of Ann Hale

Ann Hale was the widow of Charles Hale, lord of the manor of Ingsdon, as noted earlier. In her will of 1804 she left £300 in trust to the owner of Ingsdon and the vicar, the interest on which sum was to be paid to six of the oldest men and women who could repeat their catechism perfectly in St Michael's Church on the first Sunday in November. She also gave a further £60 to be invested and the interest used for clothing the children of the poorest labourers who received no monthly pay. It was intended that both payments would be made in perpetuity. The whole £360 was to be invested in public funds and the items of clothing delivered on Christmas Day immediately after the divine service. The funds, in reality, were invested in the bank of Mr Abraham which failed in 1812. Only 3s. 9d. in the £ was recoverable. By 1865, however, the funds stood at £337 4s. 1d. producing an annual gross income of £10 2s. 3d. It has not been established how and by whom the bulk of the sum was repaid but the vicar, the Reverend Palk, is known to have paid in £60.

In 1899 the charity was divided into two parts, five-sixths being made the endowment of a church charity, the trustees being the vicar and the owner of Ingsdon, Mr Bayldon. The income derived from the funds was divided between the men and women as originally intended. The remaining sixth was designated the poor charity, the income going into a parish clothing club, five-sixths of which helped provide clothing for poor children. The parents of these subscribed one shilling a month and received a bonus of 1s. 6d. for the year. This seems to have been a way of promoting saving and avoiding to some extent the growth of a 'dependency culture'. The church charity applicants were many and of a determined nature! In 1823 Michael Cumming, Richard Perry and Mary May, all aged 77, Gertrude Honiwill, 76, Susanna Coleman, 75, and Susanna Layman, 73, were successful, unlike nine unsuccessful applicants. In the early years the highly competitive contest was often accompanied by hints, exhortations and even abuse by interested members of the congregation. It is perhaps no great surprise that by 1900 the catechism was held over until the end of the service.

Bequests of Thomas Taylor and William Furneaux Widger

Thomas Taylor in his will of 1847 devised all his estate to be converted into money, invested in government stock and, after the death of one Isabella Purchas, who had a life interest therein, paid into the Candy charity. In 1904 these funds amounted to £396 7s. 6d.

William Widger was a descendant of a family with a long history in Ilsington parish. In the 1566 survey for Lord Compton a William Wyger held property at Honeywell, Frideswyder Wyger at Myll Poole, Anstice Wyger at Northcombe and Gabriel Wyger held part of the barton land. In the middle of the 18th century a branch of the family moved to Sigford and bought what is now known as Sigford House. A century later William, together with his two brothers Thomas and Samuel, lived there (and they were apparently an eccentric trio). William survived his two brothers and in his will of 1888 left £300 upon trust for the purchase of blankets and coal for the deserving poor of the parish for distribution at Christmas. Applicants had to register at the village shop in Sigford. In 1906 thirteen blankets and six lengths of serge were so distributed to the total value of £7 17s. 7d.

Recent Developments

With the increasing responsibility of national and local authorities for the welfare of the poor it has become sensible to rationalise the funding of these charities and the purposes for which the funds could be applied. In 1914 the charities of Candy, the Parish Lands, Hale, Taylor and Widger became administered under the title of the Ilsington United Charities. Wherever possible the yearly income was applied for the purposes originally intended but the present trustees can use their discretion to help parishioners confronted with emergencies, those requiring special equipment to overcome disabilty for example. The Ford charity, as already noted, helps to supply equipment to the two local schools.

IX

EDUCATION

The first known mention of education in the parish is connected with the collapse of a schoolroom over the west lychgate on 17 September 1639. This catered for thirty boys and it is probable they would be taught to read and possibly write, though much would depend on the schoolteacher. Teaching, if carried out at all in such a rural parish, was undertaken by well disposed 'dames' or by someone of clerical standing. In either case emphasis would be placed on reading the Bible. In this case the teacher was Hannibal Corbyn, described at his death in 1679 as a deacon. The day being wet and windy only 17 boys were present. At about 11 a.m. a woman passed underneath and let the heavy door slam behind her and had only gone a few yards further when part of the stone south wall which bore the roof slid away and the whole roof came down, driving out the east and west walls. Surprisingly all survived with little hurt, although one, Humphry Degon, was missed for a time and thought at first to be dead. He was found buried under rubble. Twelve had 'their heads cut and broken soe that they bledd for it to mind them all of the danger they were in. But God with their guard of Angells surrounded them'. The boys are recorded in the parish registers as David Leere, Thomas Leere, John Leere, Henry Leere, Thomas Smerdon, Thomas Corbin, John Crerose, John Degon, Humphry Degon, Stephen Tyler, Bartholemew Potter, Thomas Potter, John Michelmore, John Foord, John Stancombe, Hannibal Satturly, John Leate. Eleven scholars were absent that day. They were: Charley Pomroy, Hosias Bowden, David Byrd, Richard Smerdon, Will Surrage, Will Soaper, John Baker, Edward Leate, John Simonde, Henry Lampseed, John Gurrel.

In 1663 Jane Ford, as already noted, left to her devisees property, the rents and profits from which should be used for poor children to be 'kept at school' until they could read the Bible. This implies that there was then an institution recognised as a school, probably the successor to the collapsed room of a quarter of a century earlier. Children were taught reading only and dismissed as soon as they could understand the Bible. Numbers varied but 30 was a likely average. The standard of instruction would be somewhat basic (in 1797 *Bailey's Dictionary* was bought for the improvement of the schoolmaster). By 1865 teachers were paid 1½d. a week for each child taught.

In the 18th century no public money was spent on elementary teaching and such education as there was in Ilsington parish, in common with the great majority of other Devon parishes, was conducted in church house rooms or in cottages by village dames. Entries relating to the disbursement of funds from Jane Ford's charity show a number of teachers spread throughout the parish. From 1805 onwards there are records of Isaac Ford being the village schoolmaster. In 1813 an entry has, 'paid Mrs Ball for teaching 5 children at Sigford'. By 1821, however, there are more specific entries which refer to a charity school. This was still the state of affairs in the major part of the 19th century but the ground swell of national pressure for improvement found expression eventually in the Education Act of 1870. The Act met with mixed support and was attacked particularly by radical elements who, *inter alia*, disapproved of compulsory religious instruction and many other provisions. However, the Act was pragmatic, its main aims being to get schools built, maintained and filled by whatever means were feasible. A requirement was for accommodation and teaching to be provided for all children between five and 13 years of age. The Act led, slowly but surely, to the building of new village schools: Ilsington Church School next to St Michael's Church was one such, with a foundation date of 1873. The land, which was that of the ruined manor house, was given by Captain Hale Munro of Ingsdon. A new road was made which ran from Narracombe Lane to the *Carpenter's Arms* and the school was built on the east side. It was opened on 7 April 1873 with Thomas Lerwill as the first headmaster. Initially there were some one hundred pupils.

A suitable site was also being sought in the Liverton area of the parish for a second school. One was granted by the trustees of the Candy charity for this purpose, the money required for building was raised and a new school opened in 1879 to be known henceforth as Blackpool School. It was a branch of the Church House School and sought to provide a further one hundred places. Miss Channings, the first headteacher, had previously been teaching young children at Liverton. There were some one hundred children on the roll but actual numbers attending were often considerably fewer, a common feature of rural schools where adverse weather conditions, sickness, truancy and family pressures made attendance erratic.

Both Ilsington School, as the Church House School is now generally known, and Blackpool School have suffered the usual highs and lows. Both have passed their centenary dates, duly celebrated at the time, and are firmly established and flourishing in the 21st century.

Another school set up within the parish at Ingsdon in 1902 was known, as stated earlier, as the Filles du St Esprit (locally, the White Sisters). At the turn of the 20th century anti-clericalism in France caused religious orders to seek refuge elsewhere. The ecclesiastical superior of the Daughters of the Holy Spirit had links with the Bishop of Plymouth and this led to the purchase of the old Ingsdon Manor House for use as a convent school.

Initially the school was for the French sisters to teach in once they had acquired sufficient proficiency in the English language. Many pupils came from Brittany, their parents wishing to obtain for them a Catholic education not then permitted in France. The aims were to teach all subjects required in the French curriculum, to teach English and prepare for English examinations. Education was to A-level standard. The school mainly took boarders but some day pupils from nearby farms also attended. In 1918 there were some fifty to sixty students in all but by 1931 numbers had dwindled and there was concern as to whether the school remained viable. But a recovery was seen and numbers increased, reaching nearly three hundred by 1954 and leading to building extensions. By 1972, however, a shortage of teaching nuns had forced the closure, the shortage apparently reflecting the preference of nuns to join religious orders and serve the poor rather than to teach.

X

ADMINISTRATION

The Norman creation, or at least adoption, of feudalism when transferred to English parishes did not endure. It never wholly overturned the old customs of the community. Even the decisions of the manorial courts were largely based on the ancient customs of the rural society and judgements were given by those courts and not directly by the lord of the manor. After the Black Death of 1348 and its recurrence in 1361 labour became scarce and the pressure already present to replace labour services by money payments intensified. The parish church was a stronger force in the lives of ordinary folk and influence on local administration, which passed more and more to the vestry and to the churchwardens. Churchwardens accounts are only extant from 1779, but from early times payments made to destroy vermin form a recurrent entry. The largest payments were for the destruction of foxes and fox cubs, 10s. and 2s. 6d. respectively. Other fauna classed then as vermin and their destruction payments are badgers, otters and martens all at 1s., hedgehogs 4d., and even the poor sparrow at one dozen for 3d.! All these payments sprang from an Act of Parliament of 1565 which authorised churchwardens to make them and was aimed at improving the national return from farming. They should be seen against an agricultural wage of a shilling a day. Hedgehogs were then clearly common for an average of almost one a week was killed over a 20-year period. The accounts show that in a 12-year period over 1,200 sparrows were despatched. Today they are getting scarce and one can imagine the outcry if such slaughter were now officially blessed.

The name of vestry was applied in the 14th century to the room in the church in which vestments and records were kept. Before long this became a meeting place for the transaction of the ecclesiastical and secular business of the church. In Ilsington the court leet and the court baron existed side by side with the vestry. Unfortunately, the early court rolls for Ilsington cannot be traced and may have been lost forever. Those extant date from 1818 and are concerned with matters of no great significance. Most courts were held in the *Carpenter's Arms* and were mainly concerned with such matters as the illegal cutting of furze and pasturing of livestock. Thus, in 1818:

We present George May and others of Holwell in Manaton for fraudulently stocking on Ilsington Commons on Haytor Down with sheep and bullocks and geese and for overstocking the said commons.

We present Jacob Wills for fraudulently taking Furze and Peat from Ilsington Commons on Haytor Down the same not being consumed within the said manor of Ilsington.

In 1835 the court leet and court baron of the Duke of Somerset was held at the *Rock Inn*, Haytor Vale and, *inter alia*, recorded a beating of the bounds of the commons of Haytor Down. The commons were the lands subject to the rights of common, by which a person might put cattle out to pasture, take furze or turf, put out pigs, and such other rights depending on the locality of the commons. These were in early times, and certainly up to the 19th century, valuable rights and many entries in the manorial records relate to transgession of them by sundry individuals. (Such beatings of the bounds, in whole or in part, have continued at intervals to the present day and a line of boundary stones is now in place on Haytor Down.)

The Highway Act of 1554 required the appointment of way wardens to ensure the proper maintenance of the parish roads and the vestry had powers to levy a highway rate. In medieval times relief of the poor had been a charitable obligation imposed upon the Church and other benefactors, but when funds from these sources became inadequate poor laws were passed in 1572 and 1598 introducing a compulsory rate on parishes for relief and to provide an apprenticeship scheme for pauper children. The administration of these duties and the rating of local properties fell upon the vestry as did the appointment of a parish constable. All the officials and churchwardens were required to submit reports to the annual vestry meeting.

The civil functions of the vestry in Ilsington and other rural parishes were taken away when parish councils were set up in 1894. There was, however, one remaining function of the old vestry. So-called Select Vestries had been set up, certainly by the early 17th century, consisting of a few chosen parishioners and forming a sort of executive committee to act with the other officials. These select vestries were of dubious democratic standing and there have been many attempts to reform them. Up to the present day a dummy bill is introduced in the House of Lords entitled 'A Bill to Reform the Select Vestries'. It is never debated and is merely designed to restate the right of the House to debate the issue. The sole remaining power of the select vestry in Ilsington is to elect the churchwardens. Anyone may attend the vestry meeting and those on the electoral register may vote for the churchwardens of their choice, generally two in number. Parish administration now is the responsibility of the Parish Council acting within the framework of local and governmental authorities. The first meeting of the Parish Council following the Local Government Act of 1894 was on 31 December of that year with William Lambshead of Portland Villa as Chairman. Its functions were wider than those of the vestries and dealt with the minutiae of local administration.

XI

Economic Geology

Geology

The north-western area of Ilsington parish is characterised by the intrusion in Carboniferous times of igneous material into the surrounding sedimentary rock. Granite tors and outcrops are evident: Haytor Rock is the best known example and lies just inside the parish boundary. Most of the parish, however, is covered with the Carboniferous series known as the Culm Measures. Here rocks of Devonian and Carboniferous age have been affected by earth movements. A dominant feature is the Ilsington Fault, the plane of which runs in a north-west to south-east direction extending at least from Ramshorn Farm to Green Lane on the northern boundary. This, and the associated thrust faults known as the Narracombe and Silverbrook thrusts, have resulted in lower Culm Measure cherts resting on upper Devonian slates. Such cherts have been quarried in the past for roadstone at the Ramshorn Down, Lenda Wood and Rora Down quarries.

The principal industrial significance, however, has been the effect of the igneous intrusion. This has resulted in minerals crystallising from fluid form into the cracks and smaller fissures caused by earth movements and forming the veins (lodes) which attracted the attention of miners some three hundred million years later. The minerals mined were mainly tin, iron, lead, zinc, copper and manganese. In a simple system of deposition, tin would be underlain closely by the granite, the metamorphic aureole surrounding this containing the other metals in an order dependent upon their temperatures of crystallisation. Erosion, later earth movements and different stages of intrusion have led to different stages in mineralisation and to much variation and complexity.

Mining

Tin

The most productive tin mine was the Atlas Mine (SX 778 762) near Lewthorne Cross. Two main shafts were driven, Sarl's, which went vertically to 120 feet passing through an ironstone bed at 60 feet, and White's, which lies today in a private garden. This was deeper, driven vertically to 180 feet and passing through a lower ironstone bed at 150 feet. These shafts and cross cuts from them passed through three tin lodes, South, Warren's and White's. Horizontal tunnels, known as levels, were driven at depths of 60, 120, 150 and 210 feet, the longest being that at the 150 ft depth which ran for some 80 yards north-west to south-east. A first sale of black tin, that is tin ore ready for smelting, was recorded in 1860, with small amounts in the region of four tons in 1862 and in 1863. Tin mining then seems to have ceased temporarily in favour of iron but was resumed in 1890. A peak production of 19.10 tons of black tin was achieved when total employees numbered 45, of whom 27 worked underground. In 1891, 14.30 tons of black tin were mined, but thereafter production and employment fell sharply. In 1895 the mine was publicly auctioned and sold for a mere £300 which included the machinery. There was some minor production later but by 1903 it had effectively ceased operating. Under the name of the Albion Mine there was a little activity in 1913.

Sigford Consols and Smith's Wood Mines were adjacent and first opened in 1859 in a search for copper. This followed the discovery of copper ore during the exploration of old workings. A shaft a little to the west of Sigford Cottages (SX 774 751) and on the east side of the river Lemon was driven to a depth of 168 feet, with levels at 84 and 108 feet. Adits with communicating air shafts were driven to the east. In the same year, but on the opposite side of the river, Smith's Wood Mine was explored with an adit driven westwards. The search for copper capable of being worked economically was unsuccessful but a tin lode was found, Browning's lode, named after the mine captain, and was worked by means of a shaft (SX 774 747) driven to 120 feet with levels at a 60 ft depth in an east-west direction. The lode was at least 20 feet wide and adjacent to it on the south side a second lode three feet wide was found. Browning's lode was driven westwards in open-cast working to the top of the hill but by then showed little tin content. These mines were active in the early 1860s but there are no records of outputs, and operations ceased in 1864 when the engine house was taken to pieces for removal. Machinery and dressing plant were sold to the Bagtor Mining Company. The early optimism, not fulfilled, can be gauged from an order placed for a water-wheel capable of driving 24 heads of stamps, that is 24 drop-hammers for crushing the ore.

Crownley Park, Bagtor and Hemsworthy were all part of the same mining sett. Crownley Park lies in the general area SX 762 762 to 767 757 and extensive signs of typical alluvial methods of mining are still apparent. Many of the spoil heaps are the remains of activity by what are generally known as the 'old men'. Just how long ago mining was undertaken may be judged by a reference in a stannary court book of Ashburton dated 1684-93. A specific entry for 'Croonley' dated 1690 states the bounds and includes in it the delineation:

> The headweare of the said Tyn worke is by the north side of Croonley Tyn
> worke by a Rocke on Itter downe the first side Bound by the west side is

by Bagtor hedge descending downe wards the water leate is by the same hedge the Teale is in Croonley pitts by a greate thorne. The East side Bound is by a greate Rocke by a little old Tynworke and so downe to the water leate between the said Thorne and the said little old Tynworke and so to the said Teale or foote of the said Tynworke as aforesaid.

An even earlier example is given in the will of Hugh Bruseghe, vicar of Widecombe and of Ilsington, dated 19 August 1532, who left to his nephew John Bruseghe 'a fifth part of my stannary called the Sanctuarie and the whole of my stannary called Swynepath to him and his heirs'. The boundary between the stannary areas of Chagford and Ashburton ran through Ilsington parish: tin from the Bagtor mines went to Ashburton and that from Ilsington to Chagford.

An area some 110 yards wide and 70 yards long has been excavated around a small feeder to the river Lemon. Development in the early 1850s was by two adits driven to explore beneath the old open pits, the higher one named Lord Cranstoun's after the owner, at that time, of Bagtor Manor. Only 16 tons of black tin were apparently raised and operations ceased in 1856. To the west of Crownley, in the general area SX 758 758 to 762 758, the Bagtor mine had three shafts, Western, Prosper and Quickbeam. A northern tin lode was opened by an adit driven some 160 yards to the east along the lode and meeting Quickbeam shaft 30 feet below the surface; the shaft extended a further 60 feet below the adit. Further lodes were opened up by an adit some 400 yards to the south-west of Quickbeam shaft and passing Prosper shaft 36 feet below surface. A further part of that lode was opened by levels driven from the bottom of Western shaft at 120 feet depth and 250 yards to the west of Prosper shaft. Dressing floors for the tin ore were in Bagtor Wood below Bagtor Cottages. By the end of 1860 only 25 tons of black tin had been obtained.

East of Hemsworthy Gate at SX 744 761 Old Engine shaft was driven to 168 feet in the development of three lodes to the north and south of the Haytor to Widecombe road. An adit of the 'old men' was found at 60 feet; most of the lode above this level had been removed in the past. Several adits, shafts and trial shafts were dug and levels extended from the bottom of Old Engine shaft and at the 60 ft depth but output of black tin recorded between 1853 and 1855 was only 16 tons. Hemsworthy, Bagtor and Crownley Park were connected by a light railway some 1¾ miles in length but traces are now impossible to identify with any certainty. Some tin was also found at Smallacombe but it seems not to have been an economic proposition and by 1865 such equipment as had been bought to use there was removed.

Lead and zinc

Lead and zinc are known to have been mined at Silverbrook (SX 789 759) in the middle of the 17th century and work to have resumed there about 1757. The lodes were then being worked to a depth of 90 feet below adit

10 *Ivy-covered chimney at Silver Brook mine.*

level which was, presumably, already well below ground level. Work appears to have been abandoned in a great hurry, doubtless due to flash flooding, for the miners left many of their tools behind. That, at least, was the account given by an old man living in the district in 1852 who had heard it from his grandfather. When working was resumed, and the mine drained, the tools were found as predicted, including two sets of wooden hand pumps. Two principal lead/zinc lodes, 35 yards apart at the surface and trending north-east, were developed by an adit some 660 yards long and by two shafts. Engine shaft was vertical for 96 feet and then followed the overhanging wall of Main lode to a total depth of 480 feet. A second shaft 120 yards south-west of Engine shaft was driven to 162 feet below surface and levels were driven every 66 feet below surface to a depth of nearly 400 feet. At a depth of 480 feet it had been expected that the junction of Main lode and Western lode would have been reached but this was not so and the mine was abandoned. This was the deepest mine in Ilsington parish. From 1854 to 1856, 92 tons of lead ore are recorded as having been mined and 892 tons of zinc ore. Eighty ounces of silver were also extracted. At its peak the mine employed 60 people. All the plant and machinery were advertised for sale at auction in December 1857. Spoil heaps and the remains of the pumping-engine house are still visible.

Iron

Haytor iron mine (SX 773 771) is thought to have been operating in the 16th century but there are no extant records. In more modern times it can be dated with certainty to 1826. In or about that year a mineral was found in a large lode of ironstone which caused much learned discussion and was named Haytorite. Consensus opinion was that it was a form of chalcedony. However, it was the iron ore which had commercial possibilities and this was in the form of a lode essentially of magnetite which ran north-west to south-east and was mined at first by open-cast methods. The owner in the early years seems to have been George Templer for in 1837 the manor court of the Duke of Somerset presented Templer 'for leaving the Iron Pit open to the highway in a dangerous state and require[d] it to be fenced forthwith'. Three years before that an approach was made to Templer about a possible contract between the quarry company and the iron ore company to carry the ore by the granite tramway down to Ventiford. There were many other owners of the mining rights in this area in later years, including William Browne in 1864-8, 1872-6 and again in 1877 but then as William Browne and Sons. From 1878-83 ownership was held by the Haytor Magnetic Iron Company.

In the Haytor mine there were eight beds of ironstone interspersed with schist, the total width of ore being 16 feet and the principal bed eight feet wide. Near the centre of the open lode an old sinking was found which went to 42 feet in depth and was thought to have been dug in a search for tin. By 1875 the mine was developed from open-cast working by an adit dug to intersect the ore beds some 120 feet below the old openwork. Captain William Grose, the agent for the mine, recorded three beds of ore, 10 feet, 14 feet and six feet thick, interspersed with schist. Outcropping of the beds could be traced to the south east towards Smallacombe mine for half a mile and at the surface had been converted by atmospheric agencies to ochre. Production of iron was only recorded from 1858. The most productive years were 1880 (3,395 tons of ore), 1881 (3,300 tons) and 1882 (3,840 tons). In November 1880 old workings made long before the 19th century and part of the existing road collapsed into the mine causing imminent danger to the miners below and leaving a large hole in the road above which required 3,000 tons of spoil to fill that was, however, ready to hand. It took a month to do this and more timbering before work could recommence. (Further ground settlement was observed in 1885 but by then the mine had ceased operations.)

In 1881 a new road was laid across the fields for traction engines to convey the ore from the mine to a tipping place on the main Bovey-Widecombe road. This is now the unmade road leading from the adit entrance past the Belp Alp and Shotts to the top of Oldertown Lane. In June of that year confidence in the future of the mine was sufficiently high for the purchase of a new rock-drilling machine powered by a steam engine, but some two months later the low price of iron ore led to its closure. At the end of May 1884 a public auction of plant and iron ore was held and the large steam engine which had cost £1,200 was sold for £205. The mine partly re-opened early in the 20th century with sporadic production up to 1921. The adit entrance

11 *Entrance to Haytor iron mine adit.*

can be seen clearly at SX 772 773 with remains of a structure opposite. Spoil heaps and entrances to old shafts, now filled in, lie in private property both sides of the road to Haytor Vale at SX 772 770.

Some magnetite has been worked at the Smallacombe mine but the chief ore was haematite, occurring above the magnetite in three irregular nodule beds, the nodules being coated with black manganese oxide. Known as Smallacombe Cutting, the mine at SX 777 766 was worked open-cast in 1867. In 1880 it was let to the Haytor Mining Company. In 1881/2 adits were dug at the foot of this hill and through Smallacombe meadow which were ventilated by several air shafts. Deep Adit and Shallow Adit had levels driven from them in a general north-westerly direction. The deepest shaft went to 90 feet. Seventy-three tons of magnetite were obtained in 1868. In 1883 an overhead wire-rope line was fixed from the bottom of Middlecott hill, up to the traction engine road and near to the adit entrance of the Haytor iron mine to move the iron ore. The recorded output of brown haematite between 1865 and 1879 was in the region of 17,000 to 19,000 tons; umber and ochre were also extracted. An ochre works was believed to be at Trumpeter, a short distance to the south, but the precise whereabouts is not known. Rock Hill, Oldertown, Middle Shotts, Great Shotts and Higher Shotts were other small iron mines under exploration or in modest production in the 1860s and 1870s and all contiguous with the Haytor and Smallacombe mines. Brown haematite was also mined at the Atlas mine in addition to the tin already noted to the extent of 1,300 tons in 1864.

Employment in the Haytor area was not exclusive to any one mine for labour was moved around in that small area as, and when, occasion demanded. Employment reached a peak in 1880 with 92 men and boys.

Manganese

Manganese was actively prospected for in the late 18th and early 19th centuries, being used for hardening iron. It was mined at Stancombe, where an old shaft is situated at about SX 801 739. The mine was drained by an adit brought up from a point some 300 yards north of Stancombe farmhouse. Data is scarce on the mine, which seems to have been worked in 1879 and in 1880, but it is believed that a lode some 180 feet below ground level was driven for a length of 140 yards, its height being six feet and width four feet. Some forty tons of ore were sold. Some mining again took place during the First World War. The mine also contained mundic balls (a miners' name for pyrites) which were found abundantly throughout a length of some thirty yards and reached a diameter of around 1½ inches. The general matrix was of hard black shale. Manganese was also worked, but to an unknown extent, in Higher Brimley orchard (SX 795 768). In 1967 subsidence in a field there led to a modest exploration which revealed a tunnel about 5½ feet high and three feet wide. Drill fragments, pieces of candle and holes drilled into walls and plugged with wood were seen, as well as signs of a shaft. The tunnel was about 100 yards long and went into Brimley Hill where it is probable that the shaft lies.

Mining activity in Ilsington was at its peak in the middle of the 19th century. The 1861 census identifies 51 miners plus one mining clerk, one mining engineer and one engine driver. Some men shown in the census simply as labourers may also have been employed at the mines: one was 12 years old. While most were local men, 13 came from Cornwall. By the 1891 census only 17 are shown as working in the mines. Though nationally insignificant, Ilsington mines were a major local activity and, with quarrying, the non-agricultural activity of most importance.

Quarrying

East of the Ilsington Fault chert forms ridges in the Penn Wood, Ramshorn Down and Rora Wood area. There are many old quarries here within both Ilsington and Bickington parishes. The principal ones are Ingsdon Hill (SX 8120 7340), Lenda Wood (SX 7920 7584), Mount Ararat (SX 7976 7474), Ramshorn (SX 7902 7402), Rora (SX 8036 7436) and Slipping Stones (SX 7897 7647). At Ingsdon Hill a limekiln was built in close proximity to the quarry for much limestone was burnt for use in agriculture. An old quarry in Middlecott Wood, believed to have provided stone for the building of St Michael's Church, is thought not to have not been used since the 18th century.

The cherts, shale and limestone were used mainly for road stone, often in small amounts to serve local needs, but some quarry faces were of substantial depth, one at Lenda, also known as Silver Wood, being 40 feet high. The Ilsington Way Books contain frequent references to the cartage of stone for local road building and repair. There was also widespread working of gravels and sands between Blackpool and Lower Staplehill, with deposits up to 40 feet in depth. By far the most important quarries, however, were the granite ones on Haytor Down.

Just when granite was first extracted from here in meaningful operations is difficult to say with certainty. James Templer built Stover House in 1776 and some granite came from a small quarry at Emsworthy on the western edge of Haytor Down. Doubtless local people 'won' granite, too, in rough form, for use as gateposts, troughs, cider presses and the like. There are still to be seen on the Down the discarded remains of failed attempts to fashion such objects. Significant quarrying, though, started a little prior to 1820 for in that year George Templer, the son of James, opened a railway to take quarried granite to the Stover Canal at Ventiford near Teigngrace. George at that time was the lord of the manors of Bagtor and Ilsington. The canal had been the brainchild of his father and the cutting of it had started in 1790. Originally it was planned to carry ball clay to the river Teign and thence to the port of Teignmouth, and the first such load was carried in 1800. Before the railway, granite was obtained by surface working and taken to its destination by horse and cart along winding roads, and this would have been the case with the rock from Emsworthy. The first accommodation for quarrymen was built just to the west of the east Emsworthy quarry and the outline and the remains of walls can still be seen there at SX 7520 7696: the traces suggest dormitory accommodation. Early anecdotes suggest there was also an inn or a chapel there. One would rather favour the former in the rough and ready times around 1820.

The railway was remarkable in that it not only transported granite but the flanged rails themselves were composed of it. Cut granite from the quarries was preferred to cast iron as it was both cheaper and more reliable. Granite setts from three to eight feet long were laid end to end and left unjoined, their weight ensuring their stability. Shorter setts were used where the line curved. The line was single track all the way to Ventiford, some 8½ miles away, with branch lines to the various quarries. Where points were needed large blocks of grooved stone with deep holes drilled in were used into which a long metal pole was inserted. The wagons were 13 feet long with wheels two feet in diameter and with three-inch-wide treads. They were marshalled into trains of up to twelve wagons and ran under gravity, any braking required being achieved by applying a pole manually to the rims of the wheels. With a 1,300 ft drop to Ventiford braking must have been a dodgy manoeuvre! Horses were used to drag the empty wagons back to the quarries and also from any quarry lower than the main line, such as Holwell. Smaller quarries reached by branch lines included East

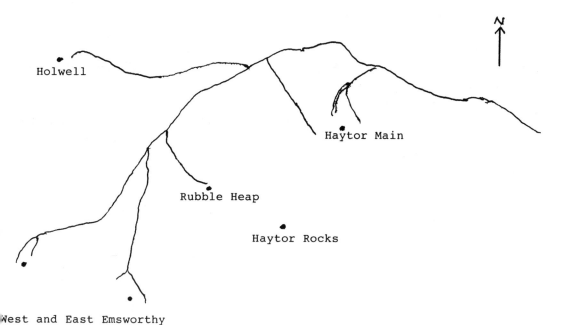

Fig. 8 *The Haytor granite tramway and its branches.*

12 *Granite tramway, lines and points.*

Hemsworthy, also known as Horra Burrow (suggesting the former presence there of a prehistoric barrow), West Emsworthy and Rubble Heap.

In 1825 George Templer formed the Devon Haytor Granite Company. It exported thousands of tons of granite a year which included, *inter alia*, orders for the Old General Post Office in St Martin's-le-Grand, parts of the British Museum Library, the National Gallery, the Waltham Monument and stone for the rebuilding of London Bridge.

Around 1826 he built 19 back-to-back cottages for his quarrymen in what became known as Haytor Vale but was then Kennapark, and also the *Rock Inn*. Workers were also housed by the quarries and an entry in the manorial rolls for 1834 presents the company for 'building houses and enclosing for gardens and cultivation several spots of land being part of the commons called Haytor Down'. The Tithe Map of 1838 shows three such houses, with gardens, occupied by William Trayer, James Clark and others not specified by name (numbers 1857-1863 in the schedule accompanying the map). They were close to the main Haytor quarry and would have been built when expectations for continuing expansion were high. One of these dwellings was still occupied as late as 1867 by John and Maria Potter and their children.

In the mining and quarrying industries demand fluctuated greatly. In 1841 there seems to have been a near stoppage in output but by 1850 all was again flourishing and some one hundred workers employed. In 1857 the manorial court called for steps to be taken to prevent the nuisance caused by stone cutters throwing refuse on to pasture near to Horra Burrow. By 1858, however, the quarries were largely deserted and the railway disused although Murray in his *Guide* for 1865 still records granite being carried on

13 *Devonmoor Art Pottery kiln.*

the railway. Decline had undoubtedly set in though, the principal reason being the need for double-handling from wagon to barge and again at Teignmouth docks. Although the railway was disused there was still some granite being quarried in the early 20th century and moved by road, the last known use being the cutting of blocks in 1919 for the Exeter War Memorial. Haytor granite was of high quality and found to be both harder and more durable than that from Aberdeen and Peterhead.

Remains of this interesting enterprise are easily seen on Haytor Down, not just the railway lines and points at many locations but also the remains of winching gear in the flooded eastern end of the quarry at SX 760 774. The remains of huts are near the Holwell and East Emworthy quarries as noted and those of a smithy at SX 7516 7724. The outlines of some of the gardens and the site of the housing near the main Haytor quarry can also be traced.

Pottery

The Bovey Basin deposits of ball clay were formed some thirty million years ago and gave rise in modern times to much economic activity. Between Halford and Liverton at SX 8105 7456 they were used for pottery manufactured by the Devon Ball Clay Company and its successor the Devonmoor Art Pottery at Liverton. (The site had earlier housed a foundry used to manufacture machinery for the movement of water, tools and equipment for use on the land, and trucks for the local iron ore tramway, which had ceased operations in 1881.) The pits from which the clay was dug were excavated to as much as 80 feet in depth. The clay was burnt to make bricks in in a nearby brickworks and some of these were used to build the outer walls of the pottery kilns. It was also used to make brown domestic ware. The pottery was working in 1913 and one kiln had been built and another partly so before the outbreak of the First World War caused a halt. Afterwards the Devonmoor Art Pottery, established in 1923 by Mr Herford Hope, concentrated on white art pottery including mugs and jugs, particularly Toby jugs, and on models of buildings, including representations of Chudleigh Church, Exeter Cathedral and the parish hall at Widecombe. During the Second World War the pottery was kept going by mainly female labour but afterwards a decision to concentrate on easily made tableware with its potentially large market did not meet with the success expected and by 1980 the pottery was no longer in production. At its peak it employed in the region of thirty people.

After 1980 soaps and toiletries were made there by the Applewoods company, but after that firm relocated to Heathfield planning permission was ultimately granted to Cavanna Homes for the site to be used for housing.

XII

WATER SUPPLY AND TRANSPORT

Water Supply

Water supply in the early years of the century was by means of a stream whose source was a bog below Haytor Rocks. This was known as the pot leat and had a history of dispute extending back many centuries. Indeed, as early as 1275 there was a dispute between William (surname not known), then the Rector of Ilsington, Oliver Dynham, lord of the manor of Ilsington, and Walter de Dukeham about the diversion of the leat. In 1826 the manorial court of the Duke of Somerset, meeting at the *Rock Inn*, Haytor, stated that it had viewed the watercourse above and below the trough on Haytor Down. This had been diverted in part from its ancient course owing to turf and other cuts made on the commons. The inhabitants of Ilsington were entitled to as much water as would flow through the trough and the owner or occupier of Bagtor Mill was entitled only to any surplus water. An order was made to fill the cuts and so abate injury to the inhabitants of Ilsington and to the owner and occupier of court barton (the old demesne farm of the lord of the manor).

In the early part of the 20th century the pot water crossed the Bovey to Widecombe road, ran through the *Moorland Hotel* kitchen garden and was pumped to a tank in the roof for the use of the hotel, then continued its course through several meadows. It appeared at Cottamoor corner, then crossed the road and ran through more meadows, appearing opposite what was then Mr Pascoe's shop and running behind Holly Hill. It came out at Struma (now Widgers Down), crossed the road and ran into an open channel down the right-hand side all the way to the village. There was a chute at Lewthorne for tenants to fill their buckets. Opposite the *Hay Tor Hotel* (now the *Ilsington Hotel*) it divided. Part went under the lower entrance, across the adjoining meadow and came out opposite the present vicarage gates, then ran through the vicarage garden to the Sanctuary back yard and appeared again at a chute at the corner of the churchyard wall opposite the school. From there the leat ran down the side of the churchyard wall to the *Carpenter's Arms* until it was lost in meadows. The other part went on down the road, the channel being obvious, past the Post Office, and divided yet again, either crossing the road and running in a paved gutter beside the

79

14 *Reservoir on Haytor Down.*

path in front of St Michael's Cottages, or running down the opposite side of the road. The two parts joined up below the village and ran down the road towards Simms Hill.

This situation was unsatisfactory since refuse and even excrement were often emptied into the pot water by the inhabitants of cottages below St Michael's Church. When motor cars began to arrive in the village the surface of the road became very dusty and this added to the pollution so that villagers were unable to get clean water for days on end. By 1902 it was agreed by the Parish Council that a four-inch piped supply should be taken from Haytor Down to Ilsington village, Liverton, Coldeast and Halford. By 1905 this had not been accomplished and the District Council was urged to expedite the matter. However, objections were raised in the parish to the expense. In November 1914 a plot of land was purchased by the water authorities from Washington Singer, then lord of the manor, for the construction of a reservoir on Haytor Down and in 1915 a piped supply was laid on, but not to all the parish. In 1920 a supply to Higher Brimley, Woodhouse, Coldeast, Blackpool and Halford was still being considered, reliance on local wells being grossly inadequate, and by 1921 all had been agreed. The reservoir on Haytor

Down now serves some 136 properties in Haytor Vale and Ilsington, and the remainder of the parish receives its potable water from the impounding reservoirs of Kennick, Trenchford and Tottiford.

Transport

Before the 19th century the lanes around the parish were used mainly by pack horses which could manage without undue difficulty to carry the loads and to cross the various shallow fords met with. But as agriculture expanded, boosted by the Napoleonic Wars, the loads carried required ever larger wagons and these in turn larger and more powerful horses to draw them. The lanes needed improvement and small bridges had to be constructed over the old fords. It was the responsibility in the main of local farmers to finance such labour, wagons and horses as were required for a number of days a year depending upon their rateable value. The rate was levied by the surveyors of highways, who also fixed the rate of pay for any men employed. The highway accounts show in great detail the repairs and new construction undertaken year by year. In the early 1800s many new bridges were built over the old fords and others repaired. In the decade from 1820 the following bridges were constructed: Bagtor, Chipley, Coxland, Langaller, Liverton, Mountsland, Trumpeter and Woodhouse.

At the turn of the 20th century the only road leading up to Ilsington village and eventually to the moor came from the foot of the hill, past what is now the village hall and along to the *Carpenter's Arms*. It is steep and still known as Town Hill. Eventually that route became too arduous for heavily laden carts pulled by horses. Mr and Mrs Bigge of Chelston, Torquay were so moved by the plight of the animals that they started a scheme to provide an easier route, with a donation of £100, and invited subscriptions. Captain Munro of Ingsdon granted land which enabled the scheme to proceed. Around 1906 the New Road, as it was called, was opened, passing between Ilsington and Narracombe woods from Woodhouse Bridge at SX 793 763 to Narracombe Bridge at SX 786 764 and entering the village from the north. Today, of course, with modern powered vehicles, both roads are used. The New Road is usually taken although slightly longer than Town Hill. The road through Haytor Vale was private until adopted by the Parish Council in 1894.

Around 1922 Mary Potter of Liverton ran a pony and trap between Liverton and Newton Abbot which provided the first public transport for the villagers. A few years prior to this John Potter, on his release from the army, started a small haulier's business based at Liverton. (A Ford truck was used to supply wood for kindling and coal for the Devonmoor Art Pottery at Liverton amongst other activities.) On Wednesdays and Saturdays the enterprising Mr Potter would have the truck cleaned out and wooden benches placed along each side with camp stools in the middle and so ran a bus service to Newton Abbot from Haytor via Ilsington and Liverton.

After a few years a new covered bus was purchased. In 1935 the company of J. Potter and Sons moved to the Tor garage in Haytor close to Smokey Cross and now the service also ran to Widecombe. Though an obvious improvement over the pony and trap, the early motorised bus service was not without its difficulties. On the steeper hills it was not unusual for all save the very elderly to have to disembark and walk. Nevertheless it was so appreciated that the gratitude of parishioners found expression, as we have seen, in the erection of a memorial in the church to Wilfred Potter, one of the sons of the founder of the company. In 1963 the Tor bus finally ceased to run.

XIII

POPULATION AND GROWTH

In 1086 82 villagers and 15 slaves were recorded in the manors which later comprised the parish of Ilsington. That number would not have included women or children and it is generally accepted that for total population it should be multiplied by four to five. So in that year the total was probably around 450 persons. In the first half of the 14th century there was a general increase in prosperity which found expression in much church building. Doubtless Ilsington, with its wealth derived from mining interests and wool production, followed the national trend. Prior to 1348 it would be reasonable to suppose that the population may have been at the upper end of the 1086 numbers. However, such modest growth as there may have been is likely to have been wiped out by the Black Death of that year. It is known that Devon as a whole was badly hit for the disease first came into Dorset and then to Somerset and Devon before moving on to London, and outbreaks were not confined to the cities.

There is no further recorded data to enable even approximations to be made of population until the Protestation Returns in 1642. In 1641 the Protestation, a form of loyalty to the King, but actually to Parliament, was initiated in the Commons when members themselves took it. A principal object was to defend the Protestant religion against popery. Some nine months later it was widened to require every male adult over the age of 18 to sign, a further purpose being to discover the number of Catholics in the country. In Ilsington, as in many rural parishes, most were unable to write their names but 174 are recorded written in the same hand (probably that of the vicar or a churchwarden). In addition the signatures of Robert Dove, vicar, Thomas Northway and Richard Widdicombe, constables, and Nathaniel Bickford and John Wotton, churchwardens, made 179 names in all with no dissensions. The numbers point to a likely total population of some 600.

There is then no data on population change until the census of 1801. Numbers from this and succeeding censuses are shown overleaf. It should be stated here that the population numbers, and the numbers of dwellings in the parish given below, are not precisely comparable. Census definitions vary slightly over the years and detailed data since 1901 is not available.

Year	Population
1801	866
1851	1,214
1901	886
1951	1,276
1961	1,384
1981	1,525
1991	2,091
2001	2,508

The picture, however, is essentially correct.

It will be seen that the increase in numbers was just 20 in the 100 years from 1801 – some two per cent. In the next 100 years there was a larger increase of 182 per cent, a great deal of this occurring in the last 20 years. The increase from 1801 to 1851 and its subsequent decline reflects the surge in the mining and quarrying industries. With the 20th century came modest building activity and a steady growth in population. The proximity of the parish to Dartmoor began to attract visitors. Both the *Haytor* and *Moorland* hotels were built as were more modest establishments such as *Ludgate*. The latter, as well as Middlecott, Pinchaford and Bagtor House, became boarding houses occupied from Easter to late September. The influx, though seasonal, doubtless led in time to the perception of the parish as a place to live in, especially as by then it had two schools.

Many early houses were owned by absentee landlords and occupied for the summer season only. But the construction of the Haytor reservoir would have been a major boost to housing development, which then was put on hold with the advent of the First World War. After the war, and with piped water available to much of the parish, bungalow building in particular began to take off and it continued steadily for the next half century. In 1926 council houses were built at Liverton (Telegraph View) and it was that part of the parish, too, outside the Dartmoor National Park, which saw much building of houses in the last part of the 20th century. There has also been modest infilling in the separate villages comprising the parish and conversion of unwanted barns. In 1801 there were in the region of 175 dwellings, and by 1951 some 375. These numbers had risen to 630 in 1981, to 830 in 1991 and somewhere around 990 in 2001. The numbers of persons per dwelling has declined from around five to just half that number. Much of the parish lies within the Dartmoor National Park, where future building is likely to be very constricted, but no doubt a modest increase in population and dwellings will continue.

XIV

Some Notable Events

This history concludes with some events of particular interest.

1275

The Hundred Rolls of Edward I state that 'Oliver de Dinham in his manor of Ylstington ... has gallows and assize of bread and beer'. It has already been noted that Oliver held Ilsington Manor at that time. Gallows were often erected as a warning to potential criminals as well as being a place where execution was actually carried out. They were located at prominent points and also at crossroads between parishes or manors. Local tradition has it that a gallows was situated at what is now Smokey Cross, which lies at the junction of Ilsington and Bagtor manors. The road leading to that point from Ilsington village was earlier known as Firchins, or Firkins, Lane and this name may derive from *forcas* meaning gallows. Firchins, over the years, has become Finchings, probably by a misspelling.

7 April 1297

The reign of King Edward I was dogged by endless wars against Wales, Scotland and France and the consequent need to raise money and other forms of help to fight them. Edward seems to have travelled almost constantly at home and in Europe. In April 1297 he entered Devon to arrange help for his lands in France. After stopping in Exeter he proceeded to Ilsington, Buckfast Abbey, Ermington, Newton Ferrers and Plympton. A study of the Wardrobe Book by Good and Orme has provided a detailed account of the King's personal expenditure and the offerings he made every Sunday for religious and charitable purposes. This and the Close Rolls show that he visited Ilsington on Palm Sunday 7 April. This was, and still is, the only visit by a reigning monarch to the parish. While here he sent two letters, one to the Sheriff of Lincoln ordering the restoration of the Manor of Skeldingthorp to John le Bygood and one to the Sheriff of London to restore fees, goods and chattels to the abbess and sisters of St Clare. This must have been a very special day for the villagers, the church and the lord of the manor.

12 April 1586

John Ford, the Elizabethan dramatist, was baptised at St Michael's Church and born around that date at Bagtor House. It is not known where he received his early education but he matriculated at Exeter College, Oxford in 1601. A year later he entered the Middle Temple but was expelled for debt. His first known work, in 1606, was *Fame's Memorial* or *The Honoured Life, Peaceful End Solemn Funeral of the Earl of Devonshire*. His other principal works are considered to be:

1620 *A Time of Life*

1624 *The Witch of Edmonton*, written in conjunction with Dekker and Rowley

1629 *The Lovers Melancholy*, Acted at the Globe by the King's Majesties Servants

1633 *Tis Pity She's a Whore*, Acted at the Phoenix by the Queen's Majesties Servants

1633 *The Broken Heart*

1633 *Love's Sacrifice* with a dedicatory epistle to the author's cousin, John Ford of *Gray's Inn*

1638 *The Chronicle Historie of Perkin Warbeck*

1639 *The Ladies Trial*

His work is generally accepted as being variable in quality. Whether he ever married or returned to Ilsington has never been established but it has been suggested that he was the 'John Ford of Devon' who married a Mary Claverton and became the father of another 'John Ford'. Unfortunately it is a common name. The place and date of his death, also, has never been traced despite attempts by many to do so.

5 and 7 January 1645

Tradition has it that loyalist forces of Lord Wentworth's command were together in one room at the old manor house in Bovey Tracey, playing cards at supper time, when they were taken by surprise by soldiers of Cromwell's forces. They threw their card stakes out of the window and made their escape while Cromwell's soldiers scrambled for the money. The following day intelligence arrived that some 120 of those men who had escaped were 'got into Ellington [Ilsington] church, whereupon a party of Horse and Foot were commanded after them, which the enemy in the church understanding, fled away'. In the 20th century some skeletons were found in a quarry towards Ingsdon which, it is thought, may have been the remains of soldiers killed in the resulting skirmish. A mark on one of the stones on the floor of the church resembles a horse shoe and is said to have been the result of the loyalists stabling their horses in the church after their flight from Bovey.

1 July 1690

The beacon on Haytor was kindled to muster the emergency army, intelligence having been received that the French fleet had anchored off Torbay. French troops did indeed land and burned parts of Teignmouth and Shaldon, but re-embarked after a few days and returned 'from whence they came'.

1750

Jeremiah Milles, Precentor of Exeter Cathedral in 1747, made a number of visits to parishes recording some of their history. He became Dean in 1762. One such visit was to Ilsington, probably about 1750. He gave one of the earliest descriptions of the parish. In this he referred to three stone barrows half a mile south of 'Heytorr Rocks', and also noted barrows on 'Rippin Tor'. He described the moorstone of Haytor Down and noted that much of the side of the Down had been turned over in the search for tin.

9 August 1795

On that date Thomas Campion, whose father was a blacksmith in Ilsington, was buried in an unmarked grave in Ilsington churchyard. He had been tried and sentenced to death for his leading part in the Bellamarsh riots.

England suffered much famine in the years 1795/6, with failed crops, a chronic shortage of food supplies and the inevitable increase in prices which follow shortages. Such a state of affairs led to riots and the authorities were nervous about widespread dissent and violence, with the example of the French Revolution still vividly in mind. The food riots in Devon and in Cornwall seem to have been focused on controlling prices in the markets by threatening the millers and farmers with mobs. It was thought the former were keeping the price of wheat unnecessarily high by hoarding and exporting. The alarm of the authorities was increased when militia in Brixham and Dartmouth joined in the rioting. The stage was set for an example to be made, and when the riot at Bellamarsh corn mill near Chudleigh Knighton took place on 13 April 1795 firm action was taken. The riots there seem to have been a rather indiscriminate affair led by agricultural workers with the aim of destroying the mill and stealing the stored grain. A force of the Cornish militia stationed at Chudleigh seized Campion and two other local men, William Northway and William Southward. All were sentenced to death but Northway and Southward were later reprieved and sentenced to seven years transportation. A fourth man, John Mortimore, managed to escape arrest despite a large reward for his capture. Campion was taken to his place of execution on the Heathfield in sight of his parish church. At that time the Heathfield was a large area stretching from Liverton to Chudleigh Knighton Heath, Teigngrace and the boundary near Stover. He was guarded by a large contingent of troops for fear the local populace might try to rescue him but poor Campion seems to have met his end without further ado.

1805

The Admiralty decided to construct a line of telegraph stations from London to Plymouth, an invasion by the French under Napoleon being a distinct threat at that time and early warning a vital necessity. There were already such stations from London to Portsmouth and an extension to Plymouth was required. Twenty-two extra stations were rapidly sited and in use by July 1806. Station number 26 was on the top of Telegraph Hill, South Knighton. The telegraph worked on a shutter system which, although rather fundamental, enabled a signal sent from Plymouth to be received in London in just twenty minutes. A time signal could be sent from the Admiralty to Plymouth and acknowledged in just three minutes. At Liverton a row of houses still goes by the name of Telegraph View. By 1814, the threat no longer real, the Plymouth line was closed.

16 September 1820

A grand fête was held on Haytor Down by George Templer to celebrate the opening of the granite tramway. A distinguished company included Lord and Lady Clifford of Ugbrooke, the Hon. Hugh and Mrs Clifford, Sir Thomas Dyke Acland, Sir Henry Carew, Sir Lawrence Palk, Mr Bastard, Sir Edward Hornborough, Admiral Ekins, General Slade and Colonel Taylor. There was a long procession from Bovey Tracey, the decorated carriages, wagons and horses trailing up the road to the Down accompanied by musicians. The Down was alive with people on horseback and workmen on foot. George Templer provided substantial food and drink and there was apparently much dancing and general merriment. He addressed the assemblage and was well received. A local reporter declared that Haytor's sod never saw before such a festive display graced by so many 'blooming fair ones'. An old sailor, one Thomas Taverner, wrote 19 doggerel verses in celebration of the occasion which contain much of interest, for example that a flag was flown from the summit of Haytor Rock, that 19 horses drew the stone mounted on a 12-wheeled car from Holwell Quarry, and that the social graces and status in society were properly observed!

> A grand booth was erected there
> To which the gentry did repair.
> A table there was richly spread
> With wine and meat, fruit pies and bread.
> Nor were the workmen there forgot,
> There was good food of every sort,
> And rich variety of store
> Which paupers never saw before.

Obviously a good time was had by all and a useful level of employment was provided for local and other people.

1 January 1852

A Methodist chapel was opened on land given by William Lambshead of Honeywell Farm, the farm where he was born in 1825. William went to live with relatives at Stoke Gabriel as a boy but returned to Honeywell in 1847. While at Stoke Gabriel he became interested in Methodism and upon his return began his preaching, which often took place in the farm kitchen. Soon after the chapel was opened it led to a local revival in Methodism and was enlarged. Lambshead had a gift for speaking and was much sought after. A respected local figure, he died in 1911 and was buried in the chapel grounds.

1863

In 1863 Alfred Lyon, a successful Lancashire business man, came on holiday to Dawlish and was so enamoured of Devon that he settled in Ilsington parish and became a major landowner. He had served in the family tea business in Bombay for many years and had an adventurous career. (In 1836 he left Liverpool as a sailor boy bound for Rio and nearly ran aground.) In 1864 he became a director of Devon Consols tin mine and in that same year rented Bagtor House and bought the Smallacombe estate. He also soon bought the farms of Honeywell, Sigford, Hindsground, Oldertown and Middlecott and tried, but without success, to purchase Narracombe. His first wife died in 1865 and a year later he married Fanny Berrisford, their governess; upon her death he married her sister in 1884. He rented out most of his properties, leasing the mining rights, and took a keen interest in the mining activities which we have seen were flourishing in the mid- to late 19th century. He lived at Middlecott until his death in 1898 and was buried in the family vault in St Michael's Church.

Of his many children, Thomas Henry, the second son of his second wife, went to Cambridge to study law and theology. His interests lay in architecture, however, and in 1893 he was elected to the Architectural Association. He visited the family home in Ilsington on many occasions and designed many houses in Ilsington on land owned by his father. These included Ludgate House, built as a small hotel, Minehayes, as its name suggests, close to the Haytor Iron Mine, Hay House and Bel Alp, the latter for Dame Violet Wills of the tobacco company. (Dame Violet gave much to the local community including the greater part of Bovey Tracey hospital, the Violet Ray ward at Torbay hospital and half the cost of the new vicarage in Ilsington.) The last house in Ilsington he designed was Yonder Finchings. His architectural activities connected with St Michael's Church have been noted in Chapter VI. He was active elsewhere and designed, *inter alia*, many college war memorials. He became Director of Design in the Cambridge University School of Architecture. In the Second World War he retired to Middlecott in Ilsington where he died in 1953 aged 84.

2000

The recorded history of Ilsington at the time of the millennium was nearly a thousand years old. Many social events and festivities, including the lighting of a beacon on Haytor Rocks, marked the occasion. More permanent remembrances were the planning and planting of a garden next to the village hall and the design of a pictorial map of Ilsington parish which was displayed permanently in a specially built stone structure at the upper car park below Haytor Rocks. This showed the principal villages and hamlets within the parish and gave an outline of the main activities, namely farming, mining and quarrying.

APPENDIX

It was noted in Chapter III that the bounds of the parish were beaten in 1785 and quite possibly before that. They were viewed again in 1797 when the churchwardens Samuel Nosworthy and John Rowell recorded an expenditure of one guinea for 'Vuing the Bounds'. No further evidence of a perambulation is known until 1967 when, on 14 October, in very bad weather, one commenced which was not completed until 1969. A further perambulation took place in 1994, the centenary of the birth of the parish council.

The bounds of the manors of Ilsington and of Bagtor have been viewed additionally on Haytor and Bagtor Downs and many stones and rocks inscribed with names or initials to denote the bounds. The 1566 survey of the lands of Lord Dynham gave the bounds of the common or waste land as follows:

> Prowces mede ende goinge Sowthward by a wale or an old dyche towards Crondell unto the landes of George Fourde esquier called Crostlondes, and from thence by the wale to the Sowth syde of Bynchen ball turnyng over in the myddes of Smalamore into the West towardes Lether torre almost, and from thence turnenge Northe goinge in a Rever being a bonde betweene the Manor of Ilstington and Omsworthye and from thence Northwardes to a Stone lyenge in Colmore and thence going North to a Browke called Halwyll browke and so downewardes by the seid Browke beneth Gretton Bridge unto a greate stone standinge in the seid water called the Horse showe being a bond betweene the Manor of Ilstyngton and the manor of Manaton and from thence Estwardes towards the syde of Great Torre unto a stone called the Horse Showe and from thence Estwardes to a wale being a bond betwene the Manor of Ilstington and the Manor of Bovy Tracy and so from thence Estwardes by the North syde of Blaka ball and from thence Estwardes to Owlacombe Borowe and from thence Estwardes to the lane ende ledinge up from a Tenement of the Lords of this Manor called Mydell Cott.

Some of the names here are not those used today but many are easily identified. Thus 'Bynchen ball' is Pinchaford Ball, 'Omsworthye' is Hemsworthy, 'Halwyll browke' is Holwell brook (although this small stream runs into the Becka brook and is not nowadays usually dignified with a separate existence), 'Blaka ball' is Black Hill, 'Owlacombe Borowe' is, of course Owlacombe Barrow and 'Mydell Cott' is Middlecot. 'Prowces mede ende' is believed to be close to the *Moorland Hotel*, 'Crostlondes' is now Crownley, 'Lether torre' is Saddle

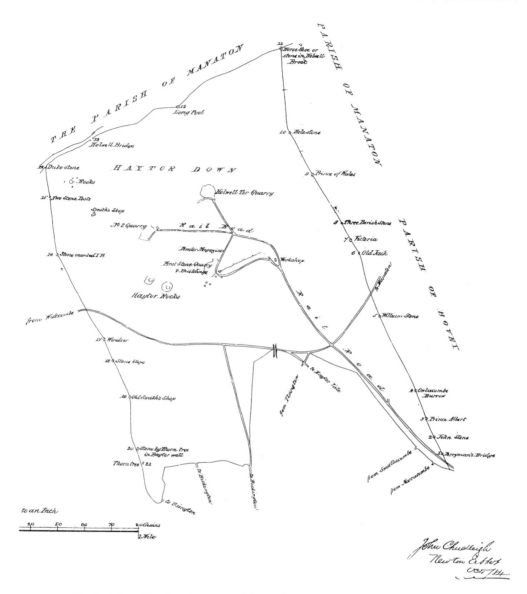

Fig. 9 *John Chudleigh's map of boundary markers on Haytor Down.*

Tor and 'Greate Torre' is Smallacombe Rocks marked on the earlier Ordnance Survey maps as Grea Tor. The identity of 'Colmore' is not known and can only be guessed at from the general run of the boundary. There is a clear error in the original with the Horse Shoe stone being shown twice. The boundary said to run to the north of Black Hill also poses a problem.

The boundary of Ilsington Manor on Haytor Down was walked in 1835 by order of the Courts Leet and Baron of the Duke of Somerset (steward William Blount) in order 'to view & perambulate the bounds thereof commencing at the bond mark called Perryman's Bridge where the Manor of Ilsington adjoins the Manor or Parish of Bovey Tracey'. It is clear from the results of this perambulation that a number of named rocks or erected stones were already in place. There is some evidence that Thomas Campion had viewed one stone at least (Haresfoot) as early as 1781. A further viewing occurred in 1853 when Mr Festing, then the steward to the Duke, had some stones renewed and others placed. A map was drawn, too, in 1884 by John Chudleigh showing the boundary markers then identified.

The stones or rocks now in place and some associated notes are given below; the figure shows their relative positions starting at Perryman's Bridge and going anti-clockwise. All grid references have SX as a prefix.

1. Perryman's Bridge 7805 7738
Probably named after Richard Perryman of Woodhouse Farm, this was a clapper bridge which took the granite setts of the Haytor granite railway over a leat. Marked PB on a small set stone.

2. John Stone 7795 7750
The letters JS are just discernible on this set stone which was in place by 1835.

3. Prince Albert 7785 7757
This was erected in 1853 and shows the name on one side and DS/1853 for the Duke of Somerset on the reverse. It replaced an earlier unmarked stone which stands by the side.

4. Owlacombe Barrow 7765 7765
As already stated, this feature does not seem to be an ancient barrow but was noted on the 1835 viewing. The present stone was erected in 1853 and marked Owlaco/mbe on one side and again DS/1853 on the reverse. It is a prominent stone standing above the natural bed rock.

5. William Stone 7711 7792
A set stone with an uncertain pedigree. Noted on the 1835 perambulation, it may not then have been named. It now has Wm/Stone on one side and just 1853 on the reverse.

6. Old Jack 7690 7810
Though recorded in 1835 it had been removed and was replaced later, again with DS/1853 on the opposite side to the name.

7. Victoria 7657 7830
A stone first erected in 1853 with DS/1853 cut on the opposite side to the name.

8. Three Parish Stone 7635 7830
This triangular stone was recorded in 1835 and bears the letters I B and M on its three sides for the parishes of Ilsington, Bovey Tracey and Manaton.

15 *Ilsington/ Bovey/ Manaton boundary stone.*

9. Prince of Wales 7600 7840
Another DS/1853 stone erected in 1853.

10. Hole Stone 7566 7850
In place in 1835, the set stone simply has HS on one side. Adjacent is bedrock with a circular depression drilled into it. Amid much clutter the Hole Stone is not readily seen.

11. An unnamed stone at 7545 7865 has the letters I and M on opposite sides and lies on the boundary of the parishes of Ilsington and Manaton. It is not mentioned in the surveys of 1835 or 1853.

12. Horse Shoe Stone 7525 7885
Noted in the survey of 1566, it was visited in those of 1835 and 1853. By the time of the 1967 perambulation it could not be traced and was thought to have been washed away in a severe flood in 1938. However, recently a boulder in that vicinity was seen to have a felspar inclusion in the shape of a horseshoe. Maybe this is the Horse Shoe Stone?

13. Long Pool on the Becka Brook 7493 7811
This small set stone was erected after the 1853 survey and has the initials LP/DS/DS on one face but no date.

14. Holwell Bridge at 7465 7763
This was a boundary point in the surveys of 1835 and 1853 and was included in a list of 1879 compiled by Mr Bearne, steward to the Duke of Somerset. Presumably this was a clapper bridge but there is no bridge there now.

15. Both the 1835 and 1853 perambulations mention a stopped-up gateway which served as a boundary point. The latter survey resulted in a decision

to put a new stone close by at 7455 7730 to be called the Duke Stone. Shown on the 1879 list, it is thought to have been washed away in the floods of 1938. In 1993 a new stone marked Duke Stone/DS 1853/FHS was put up. (F.H. Starkey was a resident of Ilsington with a strong interest in local history.)

The above mentioned stones and rocks mark the boundary of Ilsington Manor and also that of the parish. Further parish boundary stones are:

16. A stone at 7405 7644 known as Hawks' Well and marked I and B. It was visited in the 1835 perambulation. The initials are for the manors of Ilsington and Bagtor for the stone is on both the parish and manorial boundary.

17. 7410 7632. A stone built into the wall running to Seven Lords Land cairn and also marked IB.

18. 7420 7605. Just south of Hemsworthy Gate a stone built into the wall and known as Stentiford, or Stittleford, Cross bears a small incised cross and the letters RM, the initials for one of the Mallock family, possibly Rawlin, who once owned the nearby manor of Dunstone.

19. An unmarked boundstone at 7399 7580 amid the remains of an old wall known as Grey Goose Nest marks the most westerly point of Ilsington parish, the line of the continuing boundary wall running south-east under Rippon Tor. The area by this boundstone is at the north-eastern end of Blackslade mire and as boggy as one would expect.

There are also some 17 boundstones, rocks and other markers which delineate the boundary between the manors of Bagtor and Ilsington. These run from the Duke Stone across Haytor Down and Bagtor Down to a boundstone in tinners waste at about 7668 7590. Most have the letters B and I inscribed but no incised names although some had names given to them locally such as 'Irish', 'Blacksmith's Shop' and 'Windsor'. The track of these with their grid references and associated notes is given by D. Brewer in his book *Dartmoor Boundary Markers* (Halsgrove, 2002).

SELECT BIBLIOGRAPHY

Abbreviations
DCNQ: Devon and Cornwall Notes and Queries
DRO: Devon Record Office
PPS: Proceedings of the Prehistoric Society
SMR: Sites and Monuments Register
TDA: Transactions of the Devonshire Association

Prehistory
Butler, J., *Dartmoor Atlas of Antiquities, The East*, Devon Books (1991)
Dartmoor Exploration Committee, 'Smallacombe Rocks' *TDA*, 29 (1897)
Devon County Council *SMR* SX 77, NE / 259, SE / 23.
Fleming, A., 'The Prehistoric Landscape of Dartmoor. Part 2, North and East Dartmoor',
    PPS, New Series, 49 (1983)
Fleming, A., *The Dartmoor Reaves*, Batsford (1988)
Fox, A. and Britton, D., 'A Continental Palstave from the Ancient Field System on
    Horridge Common', *PPS*, vol.35, no.9 (1969)
Greeves, T., *The Archaeology of Dartmoor from the Air*, Devon Books (1985)
Pearce S,M., *The Archaeology of South West Britain*, Collins (1981)
Pettit, P., *Prehistoric Dartmoor*, David and Charles (1974)

The Saxon Age
Davidson, J.B., 'Some Anglo-Saxon Boundaries now Deposited at the Albert Museum,
    Exeter', *TDA*, vol. 8 (1876)
Ekwall, E., *Concise Oxford Dictionary of English Place-Names*, 4th edition
    (1966)
Gover, J.E.B., Mawer, A., and Stenton, F.M., *The Place Names of Devon*, vol. 9,
    English Place-Name Society, Cambridge (1932)
Hooke, D., *Pre-Conquest Charter Bounds of Devon and Cornwall*, Boydell Press
    (1994)
Ransom, B., 'Ilsington Parish and the Landscaro of Peadingtun', *Devon Historian*,
    vol. 65 (2002)
Rose-Troup, F., 'Anglo-Saxon Charters of Devonshire', *DCNQ*, no. 17 (1932)

Origin and Growth
Darby, H.C. and Welldon Finn, R., *The Domesday Geography of South-West England*,
    Cambridge University Press (1967)
Deputy Keeper of the Records, *Inquisitions and Assessments Relating to Feudal
    Aids, 1284-1431*, Vol. 1, H.M. Home Dept (1899)
Hands, S., *The Book of Bickington*, Halsgrove (2000)

Joce, T.J., 'The Goatpath', *TDA*, vol. 63 (1931)

Morris, J. (ed.), *Domesday Book of Devon, Parts 1 and 2*, Phillimore (1985).

Reichel, O.J.R., 'Some Suggestions to Aid in Identifying the Place-Names in the Devonshire Domesday', *TDA*, vol. 26 (1894)

The Manors

DRO, Survey of Lord Dynham's Lands 1566, Z17/3/19

DRO, Land Tax Assessment Records (on microfiche)

DRO, Award of Hugh Stafford and others, 27 April 1692, 57/3/10/4

Dymond, R., 'Memoir of Lord Dunning, First Lord Ashburton', *TDA*, vol. 8 (1876)

Erskine, A.M., 'The Devonshire Lay Subsidy Roll of 1332', *Devon and Cornwall Record Society*, new series, vol. 14 (1969)

Barton and Demesne Lands

Cornwall Record Office, 1593 Lease of Lands called Rowra, AR4/2074

Cornwall Record Office, 1543 Lease of the Barton of Ilsington, AR4/2073

Cornwall Record Office, 1609 Survey Roll of the Lands in Devon of John Arundell of Lanherne, AE2/1393

DRO, Survey of Lord Dynham's Lands, 1566, Z17/3/19

Hanham, H.J., 'The Seyntcleres of Tidwell', *TDA*, vol. 99 (1967)

The Church

Cornelius, C.F., 'Medieval Churches of the Newton Abbot District', *TDA*, vol. 78 (1946)

Creswell, B.F., *Notes on Devon Churches*: *Deanery of Moretonhampstead, A-K* (1921)

Deputy Keeper of the Records, *Calendar of Patent Rolls*, 9 Edward III, 1334-38, vol. 1. London (1895)

Deputy Keeper of the Records, *Calendar of Patent Rolls*, 12 Edward III, 1338-40, vol. 4. London (1895)

Jones, W., 'Account of the Rectory and Vicarage of Ilsington', *Notes and Gleanings*, vol. 3 (1890)

Milles, J., *Parochial History of Devon*, vol. 2 (on microfiche at the Devon Record Office) (1755-6)

Ransom, P.J. and W.H., 'St Michael's Church, Ilsington, Monumental Inscriptions and Memorials' (privately printed, available in Devon libraries) (c.1990)

Wills, R.N., *The Book of Ilsington*, Halsgrove (2000)

Worthy, C., *Ashburton and its Neighbours* (1875)

Youings, J., Devon Monastic Lands, Calendar of Particulars for Grants, 1536-58, *Devon and Cornwall Record Society*, new series, vol. 1 (1955)

Terriers and Tithes

The text relating to terriers is derived from microfiche in the DRO taken from the parish registers. That relating to 1636 appears on Ilsington MF 2 and the rest on Ilsington MF 4. Some words are too faint to allow transcription with complete certainty.

The tithe schedule and map for 1838 is held in the DRO.

Charities

Cocks, J.V.S., 'Ilsington Poor House in 1815', *DCNQ*, vol. 30 part 7

Copeland, G.W., 'Devonshire Church Houses', *TDA*, vol. 92 (1960)

DRO, 4932M Ilsington Poor Book 1811-1848 and Way Book 1798-1820

Education
DRO, Anon. *Memories of St Michael's Convent 1918-1971* (1971)
Ilsington Parish Registers 1639
Perkins, D., *A Hundred Years of Blackpool School* (privately published, 1979)
Sellman, R.R., *Devon Village Schools in the Nineteenth Century*, David and Charles
    (1967)

Economic Geology
Adams, E.A., 'The Old Heytor Granite Railway', *TDA* vol. 78 (1946)
Atkinson, M., Burt, R. and Waite, P., *Dartmoor Mines. The Mines of the Granite
    Mass*, Exeter Industrial Archaeological Group, Dept. of Economic History, Exeter
    University (1978)
Atkinson, M., Waite, P. and Burt, R., 'The Iron Ore Mining Industry in Devon',
    Northern Mine Research Society Memoirs, Sheffield (1980-82)
Bristow, C.M., 'The Geology of the Area between Ilsington, Liverton and Bickington',
    M.Sc.Thesis, Exeter University (1962)
Butler, J., *Dartmoor Atlas of Antiquities. The East*, Devon Books (1991)
Dines, H.G., *The Metalliferous Mining Regions of South-West England*, vol.II
    (1956)
DRO, 1689 Stannary Court Book, Chagford and Ashburton Courts, 4 October, DD
    35531
Ewans, M.C., *The Haytor Granite Tramway and Stover Canal*, David and Charles
    (1977)
Geological Survey of Great Britain, HMSO, London
Harris, H., *The Industrial Archaeology of Dartmoor*, David and Charles (1968)
Hobbs, J., *The Devonmoor Art Pottery Liverton* (privately published, 1998)
Jenkin, A.K.H., *Mines of Devon North and East of Dartmoor*, Devon Library Services,
    Exeter (1981)

Water Supply and Transport
Patch, J., A *History and Guide to the Parish of Ilsington* (c.1930) (in DRO)
Starkey, F.H. and Meredew, M.H., 'The Highways of Ilsington', *DCNQ*, vol. 34
    (1978)

Population and Growth
Stoate, T.L. and Howard, A.J., *The Devon Protestation Returns 1641*, Pinner
    (1973)
Census returns and census books held in the DRO.

INDEX